FRANCE

97102774

FRANCE

by John Laurence Carr

EDWARD ARNOLD

© John Laurence Carr 1969
First published 1969
by Edward Arnold (Publishers) Ltd
41, Maddox Street, London W.1

Cloth edition SBN: 7131 5446 2
Paper edition SBN: 7131 5447 0

Printed in Great Britain by
Fletcher & Son Ltd, Norwich

Contents

Preface

In these pages you will find a good deal of useful information about our nearest neighbours, the French.

If you have not yet met them in their own country, I would sincerely urge you to cross the Channel at the earliest opportunity, for nothing is as good as direct observation.

In the meantime, however, by browsing over, or dipping into this little book, I hope you will come to appreciate the vast progress made in recent years by those men and women who speak the foreign language you learned first.

Then the French people and their language will become less 'foreign' to you and you will have taken an important step towards becoming truly European.

J.L.C.

An Ancient People

Long before the Romans arrived in the first century B.C., the land that is now called France was inhabited by interesting people. Some have left their mark in cave paintings. The story of how some of these were discovered at Lascaux, in the south west of the country, is worth telling. One day in 1940 some boys, taking a walk in the country, lost their dog down a hole in the ground and decided to enlarge the entrance in order to recover the dog, Robot. What an Aladdin's cave was revealed to them! Inside they saw, for the first time for thousands of years, pictures painted on the walls by their remote ancestors – deer, cattle, horses, bison, all well preserved by their natural coating of calcite.

When the Romans under Julius Caesar came as colonizers, they had to defeat the brave and warlike Vercingetorix at the Battle of Alesia. Some Romans remained and were followed by German tribes and British Celts fleeing from the Saxon invasion of their own land. The latter settled in Brittany, which still has a language similar to Welsh. Then came the Norsemen, who were to harry the coasts and travel up the Seine as far as Paris giving their name ultimately to Normandy. More invaders came – Visigoths, Vandals, Burgundians, Franks, treading on the ruins of the Roman Empire.

The Dark Ages were dark indeed! Slowly the medieval world emerged. In the fifth century a leader of the Franks, Clovis, established himself as supreme ruler of much of what is now France and was converted to Christianity. Another Frankish leader, Charlemagne, crowned emperor of most of Europe in the year 800, devoted his energies to conquest and religion, leaving his mark upon history as a great ruler who unified France and Europe.

As the area under royal control grew larger and kings weaker, land passed into the hands of barons who, in return for services rendered, feued it to

Opposite: Treasures from Lascaux's 'Aladdin's cave'. *(French Government Tourist Office)*

I

serfs. Thus arose the feudal system. Warfare kept most people very busy and the torch of learning and civilization was carried mainly by the Christian Church which dominated civil life. Huge monastic orders grew up and the faithful built abbeys and cathedrals. But the true personality of France had not yet emerged, since people still thought of themselves as belonging to small groups on a regional basis.

The Hundred Years War showed this fact clearly, for at that time the King of England owned enormous stretches of territory now recognized as French, and the French king was sadly short of possessions. Fortunately for him, however, a young peasant girl called Joan of Arc persuaded him (while still dauphin, or heir-apparent) to take heart, unite his realm, and drive out the English. Though she was later burned as a witch, Joan had accomplished her divine mission and French monarchs began to assert their independence.

Furthermore, merchants of middle-class origin prospered in the cities and towns, and monarchs such as Louis XI found support from the ranks of this new class of society for his attempts to subdue the arrogant nobles. With the RENAISSANCE king, François I, this process continued with greater vigour, as barons were turned into courtiers attending the royal pleasure. In the seventeenth century, King Louis XIII, who came to the throne at the tender age of nine, relied for a while upon his mother to rule the kingdom and later upon Cardinal Richelieu who set about the task of bringing to heel the Protestants and the nobles. Continuing the good work of François I, as well as that of his father and the Cardinal, Louis XIV turned his nobles into little more than palace servants. At the same time he brought French cultural life to its highest level. This was the age when Corneille, Molière and Racine composed their theatrical masterpieces; when the genius Pascal wrote about mathematics, religion and morals; when La Fontaine delighted his readers with enchanting animal fables; when Bishop Bossuet published history and delivered stirring sermons; and when, in limpid prose, La Bruyère characterized and satirized society. Government was centralized as never before. National unity was a fact at last, an achievement due to Louis' excellent advisers, Louvois, Vauban, and Colbert as much as to his own genius for organization. This was the time when majesty could be seen as well as felt – a magnificent palace at Versailles, near Paris, symbolizing royal might and glory. There was, however, another side to Louis XIV. His wars led to intense hatred of France throughout Europe; his extravagance emptied the treasury and his conceit set a bad pattern for the future. The most glaring consequence of this was that royalty fell into a state of decadence and INSOLVENCY. As

Opposite top: Glory personified – Louis XIV, the Sun King!
(Radio Times Hulton Picture Library)

Opposite foot: Joan prepares to raise the seige of Orleans.
(Radio Times Hulton Picture Library)

3

kings became weak, times were ripe for liberal ideas and for the transfer of power to the nobles, rich middle classes and others who now demanded it. These demands reached a peak in 1789, when the great royal fortress and prison, the Bastille, fell to the mob. Once the train of violent events had been set in motion, political rivalries led inevitably to more tragedy, as the middle classes, who generally favoured restraint, became increasingly afraid of the populace. In 1793, first the king and then the queen followed so many members of their court to the GUILLOTINE, which was to cut a swathe through the ranks of thousands of Frenchmen of all classes. But the French Revolution of 1789–99 did change things and many for the better; for instance, it was during this period that the ideal of 'liberty, equality and fraternity' was proclaimed and temporarily achieved.

Alas, however, another tyrant was not far away. Trading upon his popularity in revolutionary circles and upon military renown, Napoleon

An ambitious soldier who changed the map of Europe – Napoleon Bonaparte.
(*Radio Times Hulton Picture Library*)

Bonaparte took advantage of the chaotic situation that existed at the end of ten years of disturbance and bloodshed, seized power and very soon set himself up as Emperor. During his years of office, Napoleon certainly reorganized France – the legal system, for instance – and set in progress the construction of many imposing monuments; but in fact he cared little for anyone other than himself and his own family. What is more, he brought France years of further bloodshed before his final collapse in 1815.

But the Battle of Waterloo did not rid France of the 'Napoleonic Legend'; therefore, throughout history, Frenchmen have periodically yearned for a strong leader to restore order and bring glory to their native land. A good example is Bonaparte's nephew, Louis, who in 1852 became Napoleon III and maintained this imperial rank chiefly through the associations of this powerful myth; though it must be agreed that commerce and industry benefited by his reign.

After the Second Empire and the Franco-Prussian War, France chose a republican form of government, which was to last to this day, but with occasional interruptions. For instance, further wars against the Germans played havoc with French stability. The First World War of 1914–18 caused great loss of life and much devastation; the Second, 1939–45, found France ill-prepared, despite the warnings about modern methods that had been given for many years by a young French officer, Charles de Gaulle.

The violent German onslaught of 1940 led to France's fairly rapid collapse and De Gaulle's flight to London, where he launched the Free French Movement – a resistance force in exile. At the same time in France itself Marshall Pétain led a RÉGIME prepared to collaborate with the Germans. But many French people joined resistance movements within France and, in particular, the MAQUIS gave the conquerors little peace. This sabotage by the resistance movements paved the way for the Allied invasion of 1944 and the liberation of the country.

Following the liberation, a provisional government, which had already been set up in North Africa, took over power under the leadership of General de Gaulle. However, after a period during which France began to rebuild and restore bridges, railways and airports, and to improve her economic situation, the General resigned and the Republic turned to less CONTROVERSIAL leaders.

In 1956 France participated with Great Britain in the unsuccessful Suez Venture; this in its turn encouraged Algerian rebels who, in 1954, had taken advantage of a French defeat in Indo-China to begin their own rebellion. Ultimately, in 1958 the Algerian War brought back to power General de Gaulle, currently regarded as the only man who could solve

5

this difficult problem. At first he served as Prime Minister of the Fourth Republic and when this fell, he became President of the Fifth Republic with considerably increased powers.

The Land of France

You will probably remember your mathematics teacher showing you a HEXAGON. Now, in general shape, France is rather like this geometrical figure; from the map you will be able to conclude that three of the frontiers of France are sea and three land. Of the sea frontiers, two involve the Atlantic coast and one the Mediterranean; as for land frontiers, two are mountainous, while one remains flat and unprotected by nature.

All this sounds very technical and we should do well to remember that France is also referred to as the 'playground of Europe'. In order to check the accuracy of this judgement, let us make an imaginary journey as tourists throughout the length and breadth of this varied country, remembering, of course, to keep to the right, especially after we have changed direction or are approaching a roundabout.

Driving off the car ferry, on the north coast we discover many things that remind us of home – places with English-sounding names like Brighton-les-Pins and Douvres (which the French also call our own port of Dover), golf courses and bungalows. A typical example of this is Le Touquet, which by air ferry we may reach in twenty minutes from Lydd and which possesses a busy airport catering for the increasing number of British tourists who save half a day by using this modern method. It is a pity that so many rush straight out of this pleasant town, for I well recall one sunny July day when we found the excellent beach very quiet and the streets relatively deserted. Le Touquet is in fact select, which means that prices are high for the north coast. One other detail – the airport restaurant is considered so good that at least one wealthy Englishman, who owns a private plane, flies over each Sunday for his lunch!

Equally accessible by sea or air is Normandy, so rich in memories of the last war, and so quick to recover from such disasters. Here we should certainly visit smart Deauville and Trouville; but beaches are not every-thing, and a trip to Caen, with its shining new university still rising amid

Opposite: The Map of France.

6

ENGLISH CHANNEL

BELGIUM

Corse
19

Pas-de-Calais
Nord
Somme
Seine-Maritime
Oise
Aisne
2
Ardennes
Moselle
Meuse
Marne
10
Muerthe-et-Moselle
11
Bas-Rhin
12
Manche
Calvados
Eure
Seine-et-Oise
1
Seine-et-Marne
Vosges
Haut-Rhin
Orne
3
Côtes-du-Nord
Finistère
Ille-et-Vilaine
Mayenne
Sarthe
Eure-et-Loire
Loiret
Aube
Haute-Marne
Haute-Saône
Tre.-de-Belfort
Morbihan
4
Loire-Atlantique
Maine-et-Loire
5
Loir-et-Cher
Indre-et-Loire
Cher
Yonne
Côte-d'Or
14
Nièvre
Doubs
13
Jura
SWITZ?
Vendée
Deux-Sèvres
Vienne
Indre
Allier
Saône-et-Loire
Ain
Haute-Savoie
Charente-Maritime
6
Charente
Creuse
Haute-Vienne
7
Puy-de-Dôme
Rhône
Loire
16
Savoie
Isère
ITALY
Corrèze
15
Haute-Loire
Ardèche
Drôme
Hautes-Alpes
Gironde
8
Dordogne
Cantal
Lot
Lozère
Basses-Alpes
Alpes-Maritimes
Lot-et-Garonne
Aveyron
Gard
Vaucluse
Bouches-du-Rhône
18
Var
Landes
Tarn-et-Garonne
Gers
9
Tarn
Hérault
17
Basses-Pyrénées
Hautes-Pyrénées
Haute-Garonne
Ariège
Aude
Pyrénées-Orientales
SPAIN
MEDITERRANEAN SEA

1 Paris
2 North—Picardy—Ile de France
3 Normandy
4 Brittany
5 Loire Valley
6 Poitou—Charentes
7 Limousin
8 Aquitaine
9 South—Pyrénées
10 Champagne
11 Lorraine
12 Alsace
13 Franche-Comté
14 Burgundy
15 Auvergne
16 Rhône Valley—Alps: Savoy Alps: Dauphiny
17 Mediterranean—Languedoc
18 Provence—Côte d'Azur
19 Corsica

Note: for details of *Seine-et-Oise* (1), see map on p. 14.

the cranes, or to the equally brilliant basilica at Lisieux, associated with Saint Teresa, is very rewarding. Before finally we leave this land of orchards and dairy farms, we should gaze in amazement at the work of our ancestors, the 231 foot-long Bayeux Tapestry, which tells in faithful detail the events of 1066 and is sometimes known as 'Europe's oldest strip-cartoon'. We should also visit another marvel – the Mont-Saint-Michel, like a diamond set amid green-blue sea or vast grey silt, inviting pilgrims to climb narrow medieval streets and view from close quarters its Norman abbey, where white-robed Dominican monks toll the bell for prayer.

To the south lies another tourist attraction, Brittany, where we may explore a rugged coast-line resembling Cornwall, shop in a fortified port like Saint-Malo, pay homage at rural shrines called *calvaires*, bathe at fashionable La Baule, or hear the bagpipes played by men in picturesque national costume, whose beribboned hats are rivalled only by the high lace COIFFES of their ladies. Then we may perhaps come to Carnac, where an amazing line of stone *menhirs* march like ancient warriors across the fields and into the sea.

Breton dancers in national costume.
(French Government Tourist Office)

If we do not care to travel far, we may also find peace, contentment, and good food in the valley of the River Loire. Here, in the very middle of the country, lived France's kings, when military necessity drove them south. Here they stayed during that great awakening called the RENAISSANCE; here Italians like Leonardo da Vinci came to design their palaces and pleasances on the banks of a wide river that often bore their royal progress. Here king and court would have preferred to remain, rather than move back to Paris and then to Versailles, leaving behind immense hunting lodges and châteaux that had been their residences and their joy – places like Chambord, Blois, Azay-le-Rideau, Chaumont, Chenonceaux straddling the River Cher, and Cheverny, which was one of the latest of them all. Each

A dream château built as a bridge over the River Cher – Chenonceaux.
(French Government Tourist Office)

night in the season we may recapture some of the noble elegance of these mansions in performances of *son-et-lumière*.

South west of the Loire lie the Auvergne and the Massif Central with their mountains and spas, located in an ancient volcanic region. Folk are fascinated too by Le Puy (which really means a dais), where they discover buildings perched on sugar-loaf hills, just as they are thrilled and impressed by the deep gorges of the Tarn. Not very far away, another region increasing in popularity is the Dordogne. This amazing river is 300 miles long and, in its own right, never actually reaches the sea. The climate is delightful, except in high summer when it is wet and thundery. Evergreens bloom on the lofty cliffs, and at Les Eyzies there is a museum devoted to primitive man. Finally, who can forget the Lot region, that place of pilgrimage for so many centuries; Rocamadour on its mighty cliff; or nearby, that incredible Gouffre de Padirac, 250 feet deep, with its subterranean river, its wonderful caverns, stalactites and stalagmites? A short journey from here brings the

A grand-stand view of the flock — a shepherd of the Landes on stilts.
(*French Government Tourist Office*)

traveller to the Corrèze, a land still relatively undisturbed, but gaining favour with tourists. From this region in our car, we may easily reach the wine-growing region around Bordeaux. Sheltered from the winds that blow in from the Atlantic, Arcachon's natural harbour and lofty sand dunes provide an impressive setting for regattas, while close at hand are the forests and lakes of the Landes, where shepherds still strut around on stilts. Down on the Spanish frontier live the Basques, the origin of whose language baffles the experts, while on the coast are to be found fashionable resorts like Biarritz. Here the visitor may see the celebrated *Rocher de la Vierge* – a splendid viewpoint, especially when the sea is rough; or, on calmer days, he may bathe at St Jean-de-Luz or move inland to the ancient capital of the sovereigns of Béarn, Pau.

Following the Pyrenean highway, we leave behind the terraced city of Pau, with its noble castle, its beret factory and its fair climate. We arrive at the Catholic centre of Lourdes, where Saint Bernadette saw the Virgin and was led to discover for generations of pilgrims and invalids the healing spring at Massabielle. From the forest-clad mountains of the Ariège, we cross the Cerdagne region and then climb the upland valley of the Têt until we reach Perpignan. Tomorrow we shall make a trip north west to the lovely medieval walled city of Carcassonne, set upon vine-covered hills in a fairy land rich in olives, figs, and aubergines and little changed externally since knights and fair damsels lived within its strong bastions.

The coast from Perpignan to Montpellier (both of which are slightly inland) is nowadays referred to as 'French California', because of the splendid climate and magnificent beaches. These beaches have been virtually unexploited until the present, but the French government is determined that this should not continue to be the case. Bulldozers rule supreme, trees in thousands are being planted, concrete blocks of holiday flats and hotels begin to crenelate the horizon and, above all, an all-out attack upon the sunbather's enemy, the mosquito, is being made. Only the fish will suffer, for they depend upon this noisome insect for their food.

A particularly swampy region at the eastern end of this newly-developed strip of coast is called the Camargue. Lying at the delta of the Rhône and west of the large city of Marseilles – currently suffering from the decline of trade with the former French colony of Algeria – in some ways it resembles the Wild West, except that it is flat. Cowboys, called *gardiens*, dressed like their American counterparts, ranch this land of freshwater lagoons, reedy marshes, and rice-paddies. Not only do the *gardiens* round up the cattle, but they also breed black bulls and lovely white horses, such as you may have seen in the French film, *Crin Blanc*. Inland lies the amazing ancient town of Les Baux, hewn out of the cliff-face and in parts today almost a ghost town. One hopes that all this fascinating variety of scenery will not be spoiled by the petro-chemical plant being installed on the Golfe de Fos, near Marseilles.

Travelling beyond this populous port, we come to the rapidly expanding little shipbuilding harbour of La Ciotat, the huge naval base of Toulon, the ever-fashionable Saint-Tropez, Saint-Raphael; and then to smart Cannes, Juan-les-Pins and Nice, a growing city that illustrates a trend in French life. Despite her 38,000 farming villages of less than 1,000 people, France is becoming a land of larger towns and cities. In particular, regional centres such as Tours, Besançon, Rennes, Toulon, Lyons, Marseilles Toulouse, Grenoble, and Limoges have expanded recently, but none so quickly as Nice. The reasons are not difficult to find: favoured by retired people – and we should remember that France has six million over the age of sixty-five – this one-time fishing community has doubled in recent years. But, of course, the Côte d'Azur will never cease to be the playground of youth and beauty and, as we continue our odyssey, we see hundreds of sun-tanned bodies beneath multicoloured umbrellas, that add touches of colour to an already brilliant landscape, set amid dark-green vegetation and, at certain times of the year, backed by the snow-capped Alps.

To Paris

On our way north, the car follows the Rhône valley, either along the busy left bank or the quieter right bank, through Roman France with its ancient theatres, circuses and temples. Having sung at school that most famous of songs, we should not fail to notice the broken bridge at Avignon, near the Palace of the Popes dominating the Rhône. If we turn eastwards we may visit winter-sports centres and spas in the Alps. At their foot, and graced in 1968 by the Winter Olympics, is the fair city of Grenoble.

To the north again lies the ancient dukedom of Burgundy, with its capital Dijon, famous for good cheer. Indeed the whole region is rich in fine things, but especially in vineyards supplying the world with Chablis, Pouilly, Chambertin, and Pommard, to name but a few of the wines of the country.

A 'still' from the film, *Crin Blanc*.
(*distributed by Connoisseur Films Ltd.*)

Even if you cannot dance on the bridge at Avignon, you may do so on the road beneath.
(*French Government Tourist Office*)

Further north is the land of that most expensive and exclusive of French wines, champagne. Its centre is Reims, in whose beautiful Gothic cathedral French kings were once crowned. There we may visit the wine cellars, but we choose the famous Moët et Chandon champagne established at near-by Epernay, just as Napoleon I did a century and a half ago. We are impressed by the air of opulence and calm efficiency that prevails, as well as by the miles of underground passages, always deliciously cool in summer and containing millions of bottles, lying almost horizontal, and turned a little periodically by an army of skilled workers, who spend their lives in this luxurious labyrinth.

Perhaps we prefer to breathe the 'Germanic' air of Colmar, Strasbourg (headquarters of the Council of Europe), and other parts of Alsace-Lorraine, a region hard-hit by war, but rebuilt and proud of its past. Above all, the visitor to this district should not miss the eighteenth-century capital of the exiled King Stanislas of Poland, Nancy, with its elegantly designed squares and colonnades. This north-eastern frontier of the Republic is also a country of fairy-tale villages with steep, sloping roofs, some of which are graced by a stork's nest.

Chiefly the former Seine-et-Oise *département* has now been sub-divided.

From the modest capital of Stanislas to the much larger capital of

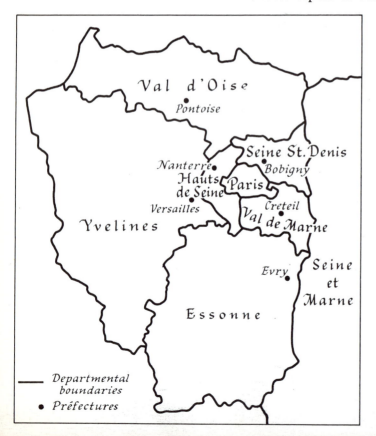

Val d'Oise
Pontoise

Seine St. Denis
Nanterre
Bobigny
Hauts de Seine Paris
Versailles Creteil
Val de Marne

Yvelines

Evry Seine et Marne

Essonne

—— Departmental boundaries
• Préfectures

several French kings is a day's journey by car, but the two hundred miles are worth the trouble. A word of warning though – if you have not been in Paris recently, you will see many changes. Apart from the sudden crop of concrete skyscrapers, the grossly overcrowded Paris region of eight million people has been reorganized into a number of new *Départements* – districts called Val d'Oise, Yvelines, Hauts de Seine, Essonne, Val de Marne and Seine Saint-Denis. As for Paris herself, she is having a 'face-lift', in that many public buildings are being cleaned externally and are reappearing in their former honey-brown shades.

Other changes, more drastic and fundamental in character, should stop some of the sprawl which the need for new accommodation sometimes causes. Consider, for instance, what is going on around the station of Maine-Montparnasse. In order to mask the station and to provide ample business accommodation, constructions fifty storeys high are going up. Inside these skyscrapers there will be offices for French postal services, for Air-France and for insurance companies, as well as hundreds of flats, a shopping centre, car park, and hotel. But green spaces have not been forgotten in this vast development project.

Another new area where they have been preserved is that of la Défense in the western suburbs, reached by an express underground railway from the Etoile at the head of the Champs-Elysées. Here there will be offices and and car parks to supplement and serve the ultra-modern exhibition hall that has long been a feature of the Paris sky-line. Another major improvement in the commercial life of the capital is the transfer of the central markets, Les Halles, to Rungis, near Orly airport, where, without CONGESTING the city, they will receive the enormous supplies, three-quarters of which come from the south by road or rail. Meanwhile, the slaughter and sale of meat for the city will be centred at La Villette, to the east.

Vehicles continue to multiply at alarming speed and therefore each year we find it more difficult to park the car in the French capital; for, having

From afar, this Palais des Expositions at La Défense looks like an outspread handkerchief.
(*French Government Tourist Office*)

occupied all permitted streets (there are no meters, so drivers put a small disc on their windscreens to show how long they have been parking there), French motorists use the tree-planted verges and the centre reservations too. In addition to all these things, to the dismay of lovers, fishermen, beatniks, painters, and tramps, the Paris municipal council has taken over the banks of the Seine, where fast cross-town motorways are being constructed. Furthermore, the picturesque Canal Saint-Martin, so well known to readers of Simenon's Maigret books, is now being covered over and filled in to make a rapid *autoroute* for the north–south journey across Paris.

The Sun King's magnificent residence at Versailles.
(*La Photothèque Française*)

Other *autoroutes* have brought within even easier reach of Parisians two of their most important and attractive haunts. For instance, taking the *Autoroute de l'Ouest* and passing through the tunnel on the city limits, we soon arrive at the historic palace of Versailles, enlarged and developed by Louis XIV in the late seventeenth century, when it became the administrative and cultural centre of the French State. Indeed, in the interminable round of celebrations and entertainments for the court, the impressive and extensive *parc* beside the palace played a part almost as important as the château itself.

Much older than Versailles, and in parts dating from the twelfth century, Fontainebleau lies about thirty miles to the south west of the capital of modern France. To reach this 'exhibition of French architecture from the twelfth to the nineteenth centuries', we take the *Autoroute du Sud* and are soon exploring the lovely RENAISSANCE ballroom or feeding the voracious carp that abound in the lake behind Napoleon's favourite country house.

The oldest corner of the Palace of Fontainebleau, the Chapelle Saint-Saturnin, appears to be attached to the Renaissance wing.
(*French Government Tourist Office*)

French Country Houses

Despite the fact that French houses tend to have common features no matter where they are located – for instance, high railings, solid gates and pretty, but functional, shutters – they vary according to the particular region. This is not only because customs determine the style used in a particular district, but also because local materials are important too. For example, around Angers quite a lot of slate is used for roofing and as layers in the walls themselves. This is because of the considerable slate resources of Anjou. Raw materials needing little transportation decide what shall be used in making houses, so, as we travel south down the Côte d'Or into the Rhône valley we find the slate disappears from roofs and red tiles take its place. In mountain regions where trees are plentiful you will find more wood in evidence on the outside of houses.

Climate too has a decisive influence upon architecture in the regions. Wherever snow has to be reckoned with – on the borders between France on the one hand and Switzerland or Spain on the other – the chalet type of house with overhanging eaves makes its appearance. In Brittany, which has quarries and an exposed situation, you will find granite houses comparable with those in Aberdeen, Scotland. While this gives Brittany a somewhat grey and grim appearance, the white marble used in the extreme south west, near the Pyrénées, shines brightly in the sun of that latitude and provides a solid bastion against Atlantic gales.

Norman farms differ according to where they are located. In Caux, a coastal plain to the north of the Seine, they are very square in shape and sheltered from the winds by a double row of trees, usually beech; in the Auge country the farms tend to be set among green pastures and have less shelter. In the immense plain around Caen, where daily battles with the Germans took place after D-Day, many of the houses are sixteenth- and seventeenth-century and built of stone with dormer windows, though the Second World War has reduced their number considerably. The manor-house appearance of such residences is enhanced by the addition of little turrets with pepper-box roofs and ornamental entrances.

The French writer, Jacques de Lacretelle, owns the beautiful small château at Brécy. Here the oak door leading into his courtyard dates from the seventeenth century and has the original locks and hinges apparently as good as new!

Above: Mountainous Savoy has chalets like Switzerland. (*French Government Tourist Office*)

Auvergne's simple farm houses resemble this one. (*Paul Popper*)

West-coast households have durable furniture. In Brittany and Normandy we find huge oak wardrobes and chests matching the wooden floor. There is a local custom that on her wedding day the bride should bring along a huge cabinet richly stocked with household linen, and a *bonnetière* which would house the lady's *coiffes*. Many dishes and bowls made of copper are displayed on these lovely pieces of furniture, and in the corner of the living room there is often a *coucou*, or large wooden clock, elaborately carved and telling the hour in a delightful way.

Looking at country districts in general, we find houses are built in a simple style. For instance, in the Massif Central (and Auvergne in particular) the farmhouses and peasant cottages are mostly ventilated by tiny windows. Inside, the beds are like those in Breton cottages; they are usually in an alcove by the side of the high fireplace, where the picturesque *crémaillère*, or pot-hook, hangs, supplying the French with a token of house-warming when a newly-married couple take up residence. In the houses of Auvergne, another traditional item of folklore is the salt-box, or *salière*. This is a relic from earlier centuries, when salt was a basis of taxation in some areas and, in land-locked regions like the Massif Central, remote from the west coast's salt-pans, particularly valuable in any case.

One final word – despite the picturesqueness of the country residences we have been discussing, the stark fact remains that more and more French citizens are living in centrally-heated flats. This is particularly true of Paris and other large towns, to which country folk are gravitating in increasing numbers: in the following pages, we shall therefore examine life in typical Parisian *appartements* or flats.

Christmas in France

A few years ago we decided to spend Christmas with our friends, the Saint-Jean family. It was obviously a good idea, because a celebration affords the very best opportunity of meeting a French family in its natural setting – the home.

As we came from the station, we noticed how few Christmas trees there were about, especially in public places. On the other hand, in the Rue du Faubourg Saint-Honoré and in the Boulevard des Capucines we were enchanted to see a large number of ingenious working models and animated figures in shop windows.

When we arrived at our friends' flat, they were just decorating the tree in their lounge, for it was a few days before Christmas. Once the children were safely tucked up in their beds, Madame Saint-Jean showed us the toys, sweets and fruit that she was going to add to the tree decorations on Christmas Eve. These would be in addition to those presents which Father Christmas (*le Père Noël*) was to leave in shoes carefully laid out on the hearth.

In the vestibule the Saint-Jean parents had also arranged a crib on a small table. The crib contained of course the Nativity scene, with *santons*, or 'little saints', grouped around the infant Jesus. We see something like this in Britain, but the addition of local officials and shopkeepers in the form of toys is a special French feature – the butcher, the mayor, the policeman, the miller, and so on. Close to the infant Saviour were an ox and an ass, whilst Mary and Joseph occupied the rest of the foreground as they welcomed the tiny toy visitors.

A Provençal *crèche* with *santons*.
(*Paul Popper*)

Later, when we were taken for midnight mass on Christmas Eve, we saw something similar in the church, a *crèche*. Then we returned home to a late supper, known as the *réveillon*. Delicious it was too: oysters, *paté de foie gras* made from goose liver to spread on our bread, and a cake in the shape of a yule-log to remind us of the real log formerly burned in French homes. Since our friends originally came from Brittany, we also ate buckwheat cakes with sour cream and drank a very exquisite type of cider.

We were told something about Christmas in Provence, where the inhabitants specialize in keeping ancient customs and rituals alive. In the south, shepherds bring a newly-born lamb to church and attend the *réveillon* on the mountain-side, where songs and music are added to the celebration. In the tiny village of Solliesville, the whole population gathers to eat bread together. Then twelve children are chosen, each receiving a gift of bread, meat, and sweets as a symbol of the twelve Apostles. After that the supper is offered to the important people of the town, followed by mass.

In large towns and cities, of course, merriment tends to be less traditional and youth takes the lead with parties and dancing till the small hours; but many of us prefer the older version.

A Flat in Paris

One summer we borrowed a flat from a French friend living in one of the suburbs of Paris. When we arrived, tired after driving through dense traffic of the capital, we had to search for the *concierge*, or hall-porter, which every large apartment building in Paris must have. However, he soon returned to his lodge and, apologizing for keeping us waiting, handed over the keys. We boarded the lift, noticing that the floor from which we were starting our journey to the *quatrième étage*, was marked 'R.C.,' short for *rez-de-chaussée* or ground floor, while the basement, where we were to garage the car, was labelled 'S.S.', or *sous-sol*.

It was a lovely flat, with all modern conveniences. We were glad to find a refrigerator, for instance, since it was high summer and really warm, but not surprised, for we had heard that almost every professional family possesses one. Gadgets abounded in our flat. We were intrigued by the *vide-ordures*, which is a chute to carry away all the garbage and rubbish. We noticed also that kitchen and bathrooms were fitted with fans to keep the air fresh and dispel humidity; that the floors of the flat were almost entirely made of *parquet* – elegant pieces of polished wood fitted together to make patterns pleasing to the eye; and that we could walk out on to the balcony overlooking the busy street.

Here we used to sit in *transats* (deck-chairs) sipping cool drinks and watching the scene below. For instance, we were never in doubt regarding the current films or shows, for just across the road there was one of those advertising kiosks, named after a publicity agent and called *colonnes Morris*.

Another kind of kiosk that we could see from our window seemed to do more business at one period than at others. Inside this little box sat a stout elderly lady, selling tickets for the *Loterie Nationale*. The national lottery has frequent *tirages*, and just before a draw is due to take place, the lady is very busy. Most people do what my son did. He bought a tenth part of a ticket and was sorry he had not bought a whole one, for he won a mere seventeen shillings!

Sometimes an artist would set up his easel down the street and, indifferent to the crowds watching him at work, would paint away under the chestnut trees until it was time for lunch.

As we left the building to do our shopping, the *concierge* would invariably engage us in conversation, telling us that at one time he had owned a small hotel in the Latin Quarter of Paris. With a naughty twinkle in his eye, he explained how he deliberately omitted to make out accounts and bills for his clients, so that the income-tax man could not keep a check on his earnings. This he explained was all part of a French device called the *Système D*, a method of making a little extra money without being caught! To this end he paid an accountant, not to get the books right, but to perplex the authorities! (We hasten to add that our merry friend was something of a rogue – they exist everywhere and not all French people are like him, by any means!). Well, continuing his varied career, it appears that our *concierge* had moved on to a stall in the Marché-aux-Puces, or 'flea-market' near the Porte de la Chapelle, where on Sunday mornings you can buy anything from a pin to an old-fashioned bed, in a vast open-air market that attracts a lot of attention. Finally, he had been a porter in Les Halles, the Paris markets, where he carried huge baskets of vegetables on his head and earned the traditional title of *fort des Halles*. He also recalled with nostalgia the onion soup, that all midnight visitors to the Paris markets must taste.

When we finally dragged ourselves away, we hastened to the shops to buy long rolls of French bread, bottles of wine and cartons of milk – which is not delivered in France – as well as meat and vegetables. And we often

Paris would not be the same without its *colonnes Morris*.
(*Philip Carr*)

23

found ourselves in Prisunic, Uniprix, or Monoprix – the French equivalents of Woolworths' stores.

A Ride by Métro

Across the road we could see steps leading into the depths of the earth and a large notice 'Métro' appearing on the arch above it. This was the entrance to one of the many underground railway stations that are never far from

Can you see the rubber tyres of this modern *metro*?
(*Paul Popper*)

the traveller in Paris. Let us, therefore imagine ourselves catching the *métro*. Shall we take first- or second-class tickets? If it were the rush-hour, we should travel first, in order not to be crushed like sardines, for at peak hours the *métro* brings out the worst in all of us. Happily it is quiet and we shall take a second-class ticket. We shall pay the same small fare no matter how far we wish to travel and no one will bother us much during our wanderings beneath the capital. If we were in Paris for some time, we could save money by getting a weekly ticket, but this would be valid only between the same stations each day; so we shall buy a *carnet* of ten tickets at a reduced price and tear one off for each journey, thus saving money once more. We proceed to the barrier, where a man called a *poinçonneur* punches our tickets, and we hurry through the automatic gate, in case it closes as the train comes in and forces us to wait for the next one.

When the train arrives, it has two rather dingy second-class carriages at either end of the red, first-class compartments. Incidentally, if we fall foul of the inspector, it will be because we are in the wrong class, so we enter one of the green sections, take our seat on hard wooden benches and the guard closes the doors.

The driver moves his levers, the electric motors surge into power and we are away. We notice that there are many curves in the Paris underground, because it follows the lines of the streets like a subterranean tramcar and travels nearer the surface than the London 'tube'. It stops at every station and we carefully plot our journey on the map provided in many parts of each carriage. At last we reach our destination, the train stops, the doors open and we climb the many stairs to the light, noting on the way a sign that tells us that our tickets are no longer valid beyong this point.

Impressed as we are by the efficiency of the system, we must know that what we have seen is in process of change. The train we used was rather noisy, like a tramcar; but, had we travelled on the line that follows the Champs-Elysées, we should have been whisked along in silent comfort on rubber tyres; and, had we chosen the line running from Châtelet to the Mairie des Lilas, we should soon have found some stations without ticket-punchers and trains with just a guard and no driver at all!

Known as the *métrorobot*, the new system is like a science-fiction dream come true. Everything operates electronically: starting, accelerating to reach the average speed required by traffic conditions and according to the number of people travelling, slowing down for bends, stopping at red signals, restarting, halting at stations – all these things are done without human aid. Of course, the guard has a manual control in case anything goes wrong, but that should not happen very often.

Under normal circumstances, the train is operated by a conductor-wire placed alternately against one or other of the rails in a sort of key pattern, rather like the top of a castle wall. Each section of this key pattern conveys messages to two receivers under the first carriage. A train cannot start until all the doors are firmly closed, the green light is showing and the automatic pilot lever in the 'departure' position.

Let us take a look at the rails in the Hôtel de Ville station, noticing the blue wire fixed with shiny metal clamps to the rails. This proves that the line is equipped to use driverless trains, which will convey you with the smoothness of a magic carpet to the Mairie des Lilas. All this will save manpower, as will the automatic checking of tickets by electronic device.

A Visit to the Champs-Elysées

The trouble with an underground railway is that you see nothing of the great city bustling about its business above you. We therefore decide to take a taxi to the centre of activity, the Champs-Elysées, that wide avenue bordered with trees and laced with fast-moving traffic. Here there are some lovely shops with gigantic plate-glass windows, smart apartments on the first and second floors and even an American drug store. The offices of the newspaper, the *Figaro* are here and the Lido night-club; and, at the foot of the Champs-Elysées, there is even a tiny wood where Parisians sit and chat or read the papers. On Sunday morning among these trees you will even find an open-air stamp market, adjacent to the Place de la Concorde, where the GUILLOTINE stood during the French Revolution and where, since Napoleon I's time, there has been an Egyptian obelisk from Luxor – a close relation of the one beside the Thames in London. Turning on our heels at this point, we glance up the Rue Royale, past the famous Edwardian restaurant, Maxim's, to a church resembling a Greek temple, the Madeleine; then we look south towards the Palais-Bourbon, or Lower House of Parliament. That elegant blue and gold dome in the distance behind the Palais-Bourbon belongs to a very famous old building known as the Invalides, since it is used partly as a hospital for wounded soldiers. Although a war museum too, it has an even more famous part to play. Under that

gigantic dome, built in the seventeenth century, you will find the red marble tomb of Napoleon I and the monument in which lie the ashes of his son.

While we are in the great Place de la Concorde taking our bearings geographically and historically, let us look back along the vast length of the Champs-Elysées to the circular Place de l'Etoile where the larger Arc de Triomphe is situated, planned by Napoleon to celebrate French military glories and completed after his exile and death. With a lift and a museum, this triumph arch straddles the tomb of the Unknown Warrior from the First World War which is lit at the foot by the 'Eternal Flame', the focal point of patriotic demonstrations, such as those held on Armistice Day each year. The arch is like a hub from which twelve avenues branch out exactly like the spokes of a wheel. The most elegant of these are the Avenue

The Madeleine, like a vast Greek temple.
(*French Government Tourist Office*)

27

des Champs-Elysées and the Avenue de la Grande Armée, but many people love the Avenue Wagram with its smart apartments and the Avenue Foch that leads to the Bois de Boulogne – an extensive park containing race-courses, lakes and beautiful buildings like Bagatelle.

Leaving the Bois, however, our taxi will take us along to the famous Palais de Chaillot, where the United Nations have met in the past, and which houses a national theatre, as well as two or three important museums. The Musée de l'Homme alone is well worth the trip, for it traces the history of man through his physical development and displays human types and costumes from all over the world. With its many fountains illuminated by night, the Chaillot Hill makes a splendid sight for the thousands who ascend the famous Eiffel Tower just across the Seine.

Up The Eiffel Tower

No matter how many times the Britisher visits the French capital, it is safe to suppose that he will invariably crane his neck towards the nearest window of the Trident or Caravelle aircraft or the Golden Arrow train to catch a first glimpse of the Eiffel Tower. This is quite understandable. Such a reaction has been pretty constant during the three-quarters of a century this miracle of steel has been stretching upwards, signposting the stars or the sputniks, serving as a television mast, or merely as a trade-mark for the French Republic.

In fact, that is how it all started, and why this huge piece of Meccano came to be riveted together. In 1889 democratic France had become acutely aware that it was exactly a century since such stirring events as the Meeting of the States-General, the March upon Versailles and the Fall of the Bastille. Clearly it was time to reaffirm France's regard for the principles of '89, especially as European monarchies – still in the majority in 1889 – were secretly hoping to see Bourbons, Bonapartist, or Orleanists back on the French throne.

Furthermore, because 1848 and 1870–71 had seen communist revivals in France, European courts had mostly decided to ignore the Exposition Universelle to be set up in 1889 on the Champ de Mars, that vast area between Chaillot and the Ecole Militaire, near Grenelle.

Opposite: A thousand feet of steel and rivets – the Eiffel Tower.
(*La Photothèque Française*)

29

Britain's official attitude was somewhat complicated by the fact that, though Queen Victoria was quite determined not to be amused and Lord Salisbury was anxious to be looking elsewhere, the future Edward VII (Prince of Wales at the time) was apparently quite incapable of foregoing the attractions of Paris, and the British public were more curious than usual about this particular exhibition.

The reason for this is not hard to find: these worthy folk wanted to see the colossal steel edifice, which, if one counts the flag-pole, loomed a thousand feet above the *Ville Lumière,* as Paris was called. For they had all learned about this GARGANTUAN brain-child of the engineer Alexandre Gustave Eiffel (who also built the framework for the Statue of Liberty which France had recently presented to the sister republic across the Atlantic).

'More than twice the height of St Paul's', claimed railway posters in London, Cardiff and Edinburgh, and if Victoria's subjects were apt to get there first, many other foreigners travelled to Paris to see this 'Wonder of the Modern World', as newspaper-men had christened it. In its first year, the Tower had thirty million visitors – just eight million short of the total population of France itself at the time. Inquisitive folk came by train, by bicycle, on horse-back, by carriage-and-pair, and, in one or two eccentric cases, by wheel-barrow! Americans even crossed the Atlantic in tiny and quite unsuitable yachts to have a look at what appeared to be 'the Greatest', and the American President sent his son with the famous Thomas Edison to inspect at close quarters this curiously elegant pinnacle he had seen in photographs.

As we have said, London had a head start on them all. To the Gare du Nord came its Lord Mayor and Lady Mayoress to be junketed by the City of Paris; and, inevitably, Queen Victoria's disobedient son Edward, drove into Paris in June accompanied by Princess Alexandra and the children. That is why the Eiffel Tower Company proudly displays to this day its Golden Book containing the signature of the greatest of FRANCOPHILES, Prince Albert Edward, soon to be the most powerful monarch in Europe. Indeed, as if PROPHETIC of things to come, in this year 1889 the Prince of Wales showed his stamina by disdaining the new lift and tackling the steps leading to the top.

It is surely fitting to add that this is only one of three recognized ways of reaching the summit. Apart from the tortuous stairway, there are of course the *ascenseurs,* the first of which stops at platform I for the expensive sky-borne restaurant, and then begins to level out as it reaches its terminus, platform II. Having obeyed the order to alight here, the tourist, already half-way between earth and heaven, joins the forty-minute queue to catch lift number two, which deposits him upon a VERTIGINOUS, glassed-in ledge. Here awaits lift number three, with visions of the summit, a cool drink, a specially franked post-card and a blustery clamber to the upper deck with its radio and television aerials and other equipment around the flag-pole.

But by far the most exciting method of ascending the Eiffel Tower is climbing by rope up the outside! Of course, this feat requires official permission, a great deal of nerve and skill, not to mention the co-operation of some dare-devil television cameramen so that European nations can see you do it.

And, of course, on the rare occasions when this incredible feat is being performed, visitors to Paris are even more inclined than usual to risk falling out of the plane or the railway carriage in an attempt to catch that first glimpse of the grand old SEPTUAGENARIAN on the banks of the Seine. Admittedly, some Parisians consider it ugly, but few would recognize their city without it, for the Eiffel Tower is more than a landmark: it has become a symbol and an emblem.

Students in Paris

At the base of the Eiffel Tower, we decide to pay a visit to districts best known to students. Luckily we paid off our taxi before the ascent. By now the meter would have registered a considerable sum and in any case the underground station at Trocadéro will serve us best. Soon our train emerges like a mole at a station called Passy, crosses the Seine with the Eiffel Tower on our left and continues *above* the streets of Paris until it plunges back into the ground at Pasteur station. We shall stay on until we change at Denfert-Rochereau to the Sceaux-line train which, one stop further on, deposits us at the famous Cité Universitaire. This is a vast park containing about thirty different hostels, each in the style of its own nation. Here thousands of students from all parts of the world live, enjoying recreation together in the evenings and at the week-ends.

The International House caters for many activities. It also contains two large cafeterias where students' customs may be observed. For example, woe betide any innocent who dares to enter these restaurants wearing a hat,

The main courtyard of Paris University, or the Sorbonne. (*French Government Tourist Office*)

for he will be greeted with a deafening din made by forks on glasses and plates to the accompaniment of vociferous screams of 'chapeau! chapeau!' until the unfortunate victim finally removes his hat.

But, enough frivolity; let us not forget that the Parisian student is a hard worker. In fact, we can easily follow him to his work. Once more we take the famous Sceaux line, this time 'direction Paris', and we shall keep our seats right to the terminus at the Luxembourg Gardens, from which it is a five-minute walk to the Sorbonne. This is the central part of the University of Paris, one of the world's largest educational institutions, and also one of the oldest, for it was founded as long ago as 1253 by Robert de Sorbon, who gave his name to the original theological college. Nearby is the immense dome of a vast eighteenth-century church which has now become the 'Westminister Abbey of France', the Panthéon, where France has buried her most famous men. Across the road is a much more fascinating church, called Saint-Etienne-du-Mont, containing the Shrine of Sainte-Geneviève, the holy woman who saved Paris from the invading barbarians at one point in its stormy history.

Upon this Montagne Sainte-Geneviève the most important educational institutions of France are situated. Clustered around the University of

32

Paris, are the Lycée Louis-le-Grand, where Voltaire was educated, the Lycée Saint-Louis, and the Lycée Henri IV with its ancient tower visible for miles around, but dwarfed by the huge mass of the adjacent Panthéon. Down the hill is the Ecole Polytechnique where the pupils used to walk around looking like courtiers or admirals with cocked hat and sword, but now are more modestly attired. The Ecole Normale Supérieure in the Rue d'Ulm is more than the top teachers' training college. It is the Oxford and Cambridge of France, in that it traditionally produces leaders of the nation's cultural life. Truly someone once said that if an enemy bombed the Montagne Sainte-Geneviève, they would 'blow France's brains out'!

We must not judge the entire student population by the idle few who hang around the jukeboxes in the cafés. Nor should you conclude that all are as eccentric as the weird specimens who dye their hair or wear it down to their shoulders. These beatniks are often foreigners, and it would be just as silly to consider them typical Frenchmen, as to decide the same thing in the case of North Africans selling peanuts.

If we cross the '*Boul Mich*' (the Boulevard Saint-Michel, that divides the student area into two and provides its chief entertainment) we shall be in Montparnasse, home of artists, night-clubs, bookshops, the Luxembourg Palace where the French Senate (Upper House of Parliament) sits, and the Odéon Theatre which presents classical drama. Like the hundreds of male and female students we meet, we may now wander eastwards, back along the Seine, gazing with interest at the row of *bouquinistes*, who display

Second-hand booksellers on the quays take life quietly.
(*Philip Carr*)

second-hand books and prints all along its banks. Soon we reach the bridge that takes us to the Cathedral of Notre Dame, that glorious Gothic edifice guarding the Crown of Thorns in a glass phial; and to the Sainte Chapelle, built originally to house this relic and surely the world's most beautiful Gothic building. We notice also the Préfecture, where Maigret is reputed to have his headquarters in Simenon's stories, and the gloomy Conciergerie, where the Queen of France was imprisoned.

We are now on one of the two islands which make up the original Lutetia, the Paris of old before the Parisii tribe, who resided here, lent their name to the important city on the Seine. Leaving the Ile de la Cité, we cross to the delightfully ancient, quiet and expensive Ile Saint-Louis, which is like a dinghy attached to a larger craft.

Walking northwards, we leave both behind to investigate the area which

An aerial photo which explains why the Paris coat-of-arms depicts a boat.
(*Aerofilms Library*)

The Hôtel de Sens – one of
the only two fifteenth century houses surviving in
Paris.
(*French Government Tourist Office*)

is rapidly becoming the museum of French architecture that it deserves to
be – the Marais, or 'Marsh', where all the best people lived in the sixteenth,
seventeenth and eighteenth centuries. There are a vast selection of *hôtels*,
or town houses, many of which are being taken over by the State and restored to their former glory. For instance, the Hôtel Guénégaud has become
a hunting museum and the fifteenth-century Hôtel de Sens has been
restored. Another ancient and beautiful mansion now under state control
is the Hôtel de Soubise which, with its partner the Hôtel de Rohan,
houses the French national archives. These in their turn attract research
workers from all over the world. There they sit day after day excitedly
delving into very solid *cartons*, or cardboard boxes containing precious
letters, accounts and manuscripts. Here there are wills and TESTAMENTS,
seals and HOLOGRAPHS – just the sort of material needed by historians who
wish to find out something new.

But the real heart of the Marais is the Place des Vosges. It was good King
Henri IV who first created this fashionable square, the plans of which were

35

completed about 1605. Thirty-six identical buildings around a green lawn began to be constructed in 1607 and were completed in 1612, when a brilliant wedding celebration mainly in honour of Louis XIII took place there. Now it has become an important nucleus of the Cité Artistique conceived by the French Minister of Culture and each summer the ancient Hôtel de Sully presents open-air theatre as part of the Festival du Marais, which offers special concessions to students, as does the famous Musée Carnavalet, rich in revolutionary souvenirs, across the way.

Leaving the Marais, we pass the Palais-Royal, that used to belong to the Orléans branch of the royal family, skirt the Tuileries Gardens, where a royal palace existed until it was destroyed in another revolution in 1871 and then we arrive at the Louvre. What day is it? Thank heavens it is not Tuesday, France's closing day for museums! Inside we come across an AESTHETIC young man laboriously copying the greatest paintings of the past in the world's largest picture gallery and have just time to seek out the Venus de Milo statue and the famous painting by Leonardo da Vinci, the *Gioconde*, or *Mona Lisa* as we call it. After the Louvre, a short trip up the Avenue de l'Opéra brings us to the Opera House, that enormous theatre where the principal dancers and singers of tomorrow are being trained and some of the world's leading artistes perform each night.

As we wipe the perspiration from our brow, we conclude that this long and tiring walk has been worth-while and that Paris is truly a city of students and artists of all kinds.

Going Visiting

Though the French are hospitable folk, we shall be lucky to know a family well enough to be invited into their home, for they are slow to take this step and would often prefer to entertain their guests in the local restaurant. However, our invitation takes us past the portly lady concierge straight into a French flat. What do we notice? First, that people shake hands with each other on arriving and departing; that this applies even to children who greet their own parents and friends in this way. We also perceive that they are outwardly more affectionate than we are and, externally at least, more polite and respectful.

Looking around the living room we see that furniture tends to be useful

A young Louvre artist copying Millet.
(*Philip Carr*)

rather than luxurious. For instance, the bookcase over there has no glass doors or polished top, as it might well have in Britain, and there are fewer carpets on the floors.

Disconnect the reading-lamp, and you will find that the plug is merely a two-point, lacking therefore the earth-connexion considered essential to safety. In France many things look a little old-fashioned too: the design of birthday cards, the inevitable use of visiting cards and the ending of that letter we received from our hostess inviting us to join her and assuring us of her 'distinguished sentiments'. Nevertheless, there is something delightful about all these things. The French have many ways of being polite and we must know them if we are to respond properly to their undoubted kindness and courtesy. Fortunately we had the good sense to study such things before setting out.

We offer our hostess flowers, as this is almost expected and in any case very suitable. She replies with an APERITIF to stimulate our appetite for the meal ahead. When dinner is served, we note that dishes which would be served together in Britain are offered separately. For instance, when we have had meat with potatoes, our hostess brings on a dish of peas. Steamed puddings are quite unknown; sweets are fewer in number and of lighter consistency. No meal appears complete without salad prepared in the French fashion with olive oil, vinegar, a touch of garlic and herbs, or without a generous selection of cheeses.

Sometimes three glasses are used for dinner, since certain wines must accompany certain foods – for instance, white wine goes with fish. Some-

37

times one is expected to retain the same knife and fork throughout the meal, placing them in a small stand between courses.

If our hostess is particularly fond of us, she will almost certainly provide an omelette and to make this, she breaks several eggs into a bowl and beats them up with a fork. She pours this yellow liquid into hot melted butter in a special frying pan reserved for this one purpose and seldom washed. Stirring occasionally, but removing from the gas before it hardens completely, Madame may perhaps add small bits of fried bread, parsley, chives or herbs, mushrooms or diced potato to that superb creation – the French omelette.

Possibly the meal will last quite a while, for our hostess has not been slipshod in preparing it and would hate to see it disappear in a trice. So we eat in a leisurely manner, discussing sport or politics with the father of the family, while our hostess prepares to serve the next course. We might in fact be at table for a couple of hours.

Over coffee, which is usually served black and with a liqueur, we find

Kept indoors, the *concierge* loves cats and plants.
(*French Government Tourist Office*)

ourselves examining French Social Security arrangements and contrasting and comparing them with the provisions of our own social services. We discover in the process that French doctors are still paid by the patient, who may then recover most of the fee from the government or through some scheme. Although the French have not gone as far as the British in providing a health service, they claim that their system keeps the doctor on his toes, anxious to attend the sufferer and earn his fee. What do *you* think?

Our visit to a French home is at an end. Being observant people, we have noticed that in France more is spent on food and less on furniture and clothes than in Britain. Above all we have concluded that a French meal is more than a stoking operation – it is a social and cultural event!

A French Restaurant

French *cuisine* is divided into two kinds: cooking in oil and cooking in butter, depending on the part of France, south or north, in which we happen to be living. Yet, so proud of their art are French housewives that there are hundreds of smaller divisions and a good GASTRONOME can tell whether his host's wife comes from Toulouse, Bordeaux, Provence, Alsace, Burgundy, Lyons or Normandy.

French professionals take their cookery very seriously – so seriously in fact that the seventeenth-century chef, Vatel, committed suicide because the fish did not arrive in time for the Prince de Condé's meal! In the seventeenth and eighteenth centuries France provided the whole of Europe with cooks, which is why we use the first word of their expression *chef de cuisine* to describe a full-time male cook. It also explains our somewhat snobbish habit of writing menus in French, to the complete bewilderment of those who are not familiar with the language.

Whether the diner understands the language or not, he soon discovers that he is faced with a formidable array of dishes. In France the better restaurants have two bills of fare to offer – the *menu touristique* and the *menu gastronomique*, which is usually twice as expensive. Let us do things in style, however, and follow the better list.

Imagine, therefore, that we are in the City of Tours in the heart of

France. To give us full choice we are dining *à la carte* and here is the *carte*:

HORS-D'OEUVRE

Rillettes de Tours (potted pork)
Andouillettes (chitterling sausage)
Pâté d'alouettes (lark pâté)

POISSONS

Friture de Loire (assorted fried fishes)
Alose ou brème farcie (stuffed shad or bream)
Matelote d'anguille au vin (eels stewed in wine sauce)

ENTRÉES

Volailles aux morilles (poultry with mushrooms)
Coq au vin (chicken in wine sauce)
Marcassin de Sologne (wild boar)
Escalopes à la crème (veal in cream sauce)
Caneton aux petits pois (duckling with peas)

LÉGUMES

Choux-verts au beurre (cabbage with butter)
Salade verte
Asperges (asparagus)
Champignons farcis (stuffed mushrooms)

FROMAGES

Olivet bleu ou à la cendre (blue Olivet or in ashes)
Vendôme (goat's milk cheese)
Sainte-Maure
Crémets frais (Anjou cream cheese)

FRUITS

Fraises de Saumur (strawberries)
Pommes reinettes (pippin apples)
Abricots et poires d'Angers (apricots and pears)

DESSERTS

Gâteau aux amandes (almond cake)
Chaussons aux prunes (plum turnovers)
Cotignac d'Orléans (quince jelly)
Pâtisseries de Tours (assorted pastries)
Sucre d'orge (barley-sugar)

This gorgeous and bewildering choice of food would be washed down with local wines. Red wines for the *entrée* and cheese courses from Bourgueil and Chinon, or rosé wine from Anjou; white wines for the rest from Vouvray, Saumur and the Coteaux du Layon. Of course you can always order mineral water instead and this means precisely what it says; the French drink a great deal of spa water from various parts of France. Again, if the local cheeses do not suit our palate, France has many varieties to offer the traveller! For instance, there is Gruyère which comes from the eastern provinces and has holes in it; Cantal from the Massif Central; Reblochon, from the Alps; Roquefort, a blue cheese made in south-west France from ewe's milk; Livarot and Camembert from Normandy; Fondue de Savoie, covered in grape seeds: Brie, made from very rich milk; Pont l'Évêque, square in shape from Normandy; Carré de l'Est, also square but originating in Champagne; Chèvre, made from goat's milk, and 267 others!

Paying the bill, we must not forget the tip. Careful, though! Is it really necessary? Already several restaurant firms have either abolished gratuities or included them in the price of the meal, so it is always as well to ask: 'Le service est compris?' Tipping is a nasty relic of days before men and women had acquired their independence and ceased to be serfs. Yet republican France clings to this bad system, and you will be expected to hand a franc to the chap who cuts your hair, another to your taxi-driver, fifty centimes to the lady who shows you to your seat in the theatre or cinema, and more if you can afford a better seat, a more individual hair cut or a longer taxi journey! So please do not tip more than you need!

41

How France is Governed

The Assemblée Nationale, or Lower House of Parliament.
(*Philip Carr*)

On the morning of April 21, 1967, two members of the French Parliament were facing each other in their shirt sleeves and with drawn *épées* in their hands. It appears that M. Defferre, socialist mayor of Marseilles had slandered M. Ribière, a supporter of General de Gaulle and had subsequently refused to withdraw the remark, at which point M. Ribière had challenged his enemy to a duel. Having taken some last-minute fencing lessons in the parliamentary gymnasium – neither men had previously handled the dangerous *épéé* which the offended party deliberately selected as being a 'noble weapon' – M. Ribière arrived with his seconds to meet M. Defferre and to draw blood. He was disappointed; it was his opponent who drew first and second blood (scratches on the arm); so the whole thing was called off, since honour was duly satisfied. Duels are, of course, forbidden by French law these days and French politicians have more normal and peaceful means of airing their grievances.

An essential preliminary, of course, is to seek election. In every *arrondissement* each citizen over the age of twenty-one uses his vote to elect a *député* (M.P.) to the *Assemblée Nationale* (House of Commons). This Assembly is elected by UNIVERSAL SUFFRAGE for a period of five years and

42

any French citizen over the age of twenty-three can offer himself as a candidate. There are nearly five hundred members in the Lower House of Parliament. Seated around a semi-circular hall, they initiate laws and vote upon *projets de loi* (government bills) or *propositions de loi* (private members' bills), by turning a key connected to an electronic counter, a system which is certainly more modern than the British arrangement of division-lobbies and tellers.

The Upper House, or *Sénat*, has so far been deemed to be a stabilizing factor in government, since it could apply the brake to legislation. All this is changing in certain ways. Since the riots and strikes of May–June 1968, President de Gaulle has proposed to have the Senate (merged with the Conseil Economique) represent commercial, financial and syndicalist (trade-unions) interests and thus turn from checking the Assembly towards becoming a consultative body.

However, the most important and powerful force in French government today is the President of the Republic, who can be compared with his American counterpart. President de Gaulle was in office first for seven years and in December 1965 was re-elected by direct, universal suffrage. He has taken full advantage of his constitutional right to choose the Prime Minister. He has not only RATIFIED treaties and ACCREDITED ambassadors, taken emergency powers to ensure order when it is threatened, but he has generally behaved as though he personified the spirit and will of the French people as a whole. For instance, traditionally the Prime Minister has the right to select his ministers, who are then nominated by the President of the Republic. However, French socialists have pointed out that recently this selection has been performed entirely by the President. Thanks, nevertheless, to this veiled AUTOCRACY, France has at last achieved stability despite the disturbances of mid-1968.

The chief ministries of State are Foreign Affairs (on the Quai d'Orsay), the Ministry of the Interior, or Home Office, the Ministry of Finance, the Ministry of National Education, the Ministry of Agriculture, the Ministry of Justice and the Ministry of National Defence, all centred in Paris.

Important, however, as the French government is, we must not forget the crucial role played in political life by regional organization. The smallest unit of French local organization is called a *commune*. This is what the Americans would call a 'neighbourhood unit', formed because people happen to reside in one given area and have interests in common. So each *commune* is very much a community, which makes the word easy to remember too.

The area occupied by any *commune* varies very much from place to

place: towns possess larger *communes* than rural districts. With its 19,000 inhabitants, for example, Fontainebleau, thirty miles or so to the south east, occupies an area greater than Paris with its closely packed millions; but the majority of *communes* are very small. The proof of this is that there are about 38,000 *communes*: 800 *communes* have less than fifty inhabitants, and 3,423 less than a hundred.

These diverse and different units have two principal, linked institutions: first, the *conseil municipal* (municipal council) which has regular meetings to decide what shall be done in the interests of the community; second, the mayor, with his assistants called *adjoints*, who put into effect council decisions but also represent the French government. That is why the mayor's office is always adorned with a photograph of the President of the Republic.

The Centre of the Commune

On July 14, France celebrates the Fall of the Bastille. It is great fun to take one of those green Paris buses – on this day surmounted by tricolour flags – as far as a small town, just beyond the limit of the capital, called Gentilly. You buy a book of tiny tickets from the conductor, ask him how many sections are required for your journey and hand them over to be stamped.

Arriving in Gentilly, you would hardly imagine that such a place could be within hailing distance of Paris. In front of the flag-bedecked *mairie* (town hall) a wooden stage has been erected and, as the sun goes down, musicians with accordions, saxophones and drums take their places on the stone steps behind this platform. When the music begins, all the couples who have been assembling in the square take to the trestle platform and dance all night in front of their *mairie* – which proves that this is the focal point of community life.

Not only do people go there to marry, to register births or record deaths – every married couple receives a *livret* (a little book), in which such things are set down – when they buy a house or land, they must also apply to the *mairie*. This is because, throughout France, the commune holds the register of the general allocation and possession of land. This register or general

Opposite: President de Gaulle in official dress. This portrait adorns many French *mairies*. (*Keystone Press Agency*)

45

plan is called a *cadastre*. In the *cadastre* plots of land and the use to which they are put are indicated on a large-scale map and there is also a list of owners. The *cadastre* helps the taxation authorities to be fair in their assessment of land tax.

The local *agents de police* are also under the mayor's control and at his disposal. These are the policeman who, like GENDARMES, wear a *képi* or small round cap with a neb, but, unlike gendarmes (who live in barracks and are national) reside at home with their wives and families. The *agents* carry a white baton with which they direct the traffic in towns; GENDARMES undertake this job less often, since they are in country districts more often than in towns. Another kind of national police, the C.R.S. or riot squads, usually wear a kind of battle-dress, gaiters and a flat, blue uniform cap to match the rest of their outfit but, when quelling riots, are dressed more like soldiers. Since they must avoid fraternizing with the public, they are never drawn from the region in which they operate.

Firemen too are under the mayor's control. In small places, they are volunteers and part-time entertainers; but in the towns the *sapeurs-pompiers* find less energy to devote to providing village music, for they are organized like a branch of the army and, in time of war, serve as sappers – hence the double name.

Centred in the *mairie* are many services: public health and cleansing, for instance. (On payment of a fee you can have your dustbins emptied every day except Sunday.) Under the control of this important building come the band of dedicated workers who, in large towns, and by means of rolls of sacking, direct streams of clean water down the gutters to wash the sides of the streets. The municipal staff also keeps an eye on smoke abatement, water supplies, urban heating (often from a central plant), market stalls, and gas and electricity distribution from nationalized sources.

The mayor's staff also control public transport (such as it is), hospital facilities, old people's homes, day nurseries, clinics, *colonies de vacances* (children's holiday camps), unemployment and funeral arrangements.

The mayor and his *adjoints* are elected by the municipal council, of which they are of course members. The municipal council is chosen every six years by members of the *commune* entitled to vote and since the Second World War this includes women too. The number of council members varies from nine to thirty-seven according to the size of the area. The council is convened four times a year, in February, May, August, and November, but it also meets when the mayor considers it should or when one-third of its members ask for a special meeting. It may also be called by the head of the department or his deputy – that is, by the *Préfet* or *Sous-Préfet*.

Opposite: In combat uniform, C.R.S. in action against students, May 1968.
(*United Press International*)

46

We have seen that French couples go to the *mairie* to get married. This however, is merely the civil wedding and, in most cases, a church ceremony follows. Often the bride and her father lead the wedding procession on foot to the church, the bridegroom bringing up the rear with the bride's mother. Perhaps you will find him in a dinner jacket with a black bow-tie, whilst his already *legally* acknowledged wife has put on her white bridal gown and veil. Between them there will be the double file of guests.

When the church service is at an end, a reception is held locally and presents are viewed. But soon the whole party takes off for one or more days of junketing and revelry at some country inn, where they may meet up with other wedding parties doing the same thing. In this way the honeymoon can be postponed for some hours and the guests make a long week-end of the celebrations before they return to their own homes.

A French School

One year we stayed in a French country town in the very centre of a farming area. The hotel owner had a son, aged about fourteen, who told me quite a lot about his secondary school.

Some things, of course, one did not need to ask; for example, the fact that he left home each day about half past seven confirmed the rumour that French children begin lessons about eight o'clock in the morning, when some of us are only just waking up. We noticed too that he appeared to have a long lunch-break (twelve noon till two) and that he returned home about four thirty. More often than not he had Saturday afternoon, and always Thursday afternoon free.

He willingly filled in the remaining details. His was a large *lycée* with three thousand boys, many of whom were resident and known formally as *internes*. At week-ends we saw them in crocodile formation walking through the town. They were accompanied and supervised by a *pion* (*maître d'étu-des*), a student from the nearby university, who worked at the school in a number of routine capacities in order to make ends meet and to supplement his grant. For example, it was one of these *pions* who saw the boys to bed at night after he had kept an eye on them during detention (*retenue*) and what we call 'prep'. Lights-out took place about nine, said our young informant.

There are two types of *pions*: *maîtres d'internat* who supervise 'prep'

48

and dormitories; and *maîtres d'externat* who help with day-study and discipline. There are also *adjoints* who, while still young and responsible for supervisory duties, have taken their first degree (*licence*) and are preparing themselves for the special schoolmaster's qualification, the *agrégation*. The *agrégés* themselves, the *professeurs*, come at the very top of the HIERARCHY, arriving for lessons at fixed hours and then departing, leaving others to cope with activities outside or inside the school. This imparts to the French secondary system its scholarly bias; boarding pupils in our friend's establishment put in eleven hours of study each working day!

The principal of the school was called the *proviseur* and was assisted in organizing things by an *économe*, who looked after finance, and an *intendant* who attended to everyday problems, like laundry, supervision of cleaners, and ordering food.

Discipline was maintained by a *censeur* and *surveillant-général*, the former being also concerned with time-tabling. Caning was almost unknown, but the setting of extra work in the form of exercises and essays was all too common as end of term drew near.

Holidays were fairly short in December-January (about twelve days) and at Easter (about a fortnight), but in summer they extended from the end of

A lycée in Paris.
(Keystone Press Agency)

June until September. Still, since many a French family seems to have two houses, this is no hardship. The wealthier ones go abroad or take foreign students into their homes on an *au pair* basis – that is, living with the family and receiving pocket money and keep. Others arrange an exchange so that their son or daughter may spend some time in a family overseas or in other parts of Europe, to learn the language.

I once asked our young friend whether there was much P.T. and his reply was that only occasional, and fairly short periods were allocated to physical activities, though there is now a gymnasium test in the *baccalauréat* – the examination often known as the *bac.* or *bachot* and equivalent to our G.C.E. or leaving certificates.

If P.T. is still less important in France than in Britain, certain subjects have a more satisfactory place in French programmes: first, use of the mother tongue is stimulated by oral and written work to an extent unknown in Britain; secondly citizenship, or the teaching of one's duties to the community or State, is more developed and widespread; finally, moral tuition through ethics and philosophy figures more largely in the syllabus.

Though our host's son came home regularly for his mid-day meal, many of his friends and of course those who were resident stayed to lunch. This is plain but very adequate, beginning with a good helping of homely soup or cold sausage, followed by some kind of meat every day except Friday, when fish (cod) is served. Vegetables follow separately, though pupils are expected to use the same plate and keep their knife and fork. Finally, as dessert, there may be a banana or an orange. Water is drunk, occasionally with a little red wine. Coffee is not served to pupils, but only to members of the staff.

Extra-curricular activities are less numerous than in Britain, though this school possessed a photographic club, a chess club, and a stamp collectors' circle. On the whole the working day, consisting mainly of study, made outside activities difficult, though older boys played basket-ball in the playground.

Before the First World War (1914–18), children at French schools wore a sort of uniform cap; after 1918 and until the Second World War (1939–45) they often sported a kind of brown smock or *sarrau* in the lower school. Now any uniform is rare.

Our proprietor's son, Jacques, told us that he was about to enter what is called the 'Second Cycle' in French education. This cycle involves pupils between the ages of fifteen and eighteen and has recently been reformed. The purpose of the reform has been given as firstly, to democratize education, so that in fact schools become almost comprehensive in their character; secondly, the French desire an education system that is less PEDANTIC and more technological; thirdly, they consider that the new arrangement will best meet the needs of the swollen school population and counteract the shortage of teachers.

Of the fifty million Frenchmen and women, sixteen million are under the age of twenty and in a few years' time they will constitute over half the population. So education is tremendously important in modern France.

Odd Facts about Education

Here are a few additional interesting facts about school life across the Channel. Did you know that in French secondary schools it is unusual to find boys and girls taught together; or that many more French children within the state system attend boarding schools than in Britain? School

Girls attend their own separate lycée. Do you agree with co-education?
(Keystone Press Agency)

buses are almost unknown in France, and, in any case, in a big country with relatively few towns it is considered best to have the children residing in quite large schools – one *lycée* in Brest has about 5,000 pupils – where all their attention can be focused on work and no time lost in travel.

Did you realize that French teachers as a whole are more respected by the community than are their British counterparts? Did you know that French school inspectors are proud to inform you that, at a given hour, all schools throughout the Republic will be learning the same things in equivalent classes? Did you know that French parents are expected to take a great interest in their children's homework and have to sign a book stating that they have properly supervised it? Parents consider that homework is good for children and thoroughly approve of it! Did you know that in France education is free and 80 per cent state-controlled? In state schools there is no religious instruction, for Church and State were separated in 1905.

Do you know what *classes de neige* are? Yes, every year thousands of boys and girls spend about a month at some winter sports centre. In the mornings they have lessons as usual; but after lunch they fill their lungs with pure mountain air as they skate or ski under expert tuition and the cost of all this is mainly met by the Government and local authorities. Although in France the local authorities play a smaller role in the administration of education than they do in England, each *commune* must build at least one school which remains its own property, but it may also supply a nursery and a college of general education – usually with State assistance if the project is costly. Generally speaking, *lycées* (the supreme form of secondary school) are the responsibility of the State, but the towns participate in their construction.

Did you know that, just as British university students have a 'rag' at the end of their studies, French children indulge in a little uproariousness called the *monôme*, a noisy procession through the streets to let everyone know that term is over? I was once standing in front of the magnificent château of Versailles, when waves of teenagers began to break all around me and shouts of 'Au château!' assailed my ears; but, thanks to police vigilance, the whole thing passed off hilariously and no one actually penetrated beyond the wrought-iron railings of the palace!

Incidentally, a similar demonstration of high spirits occurs before the young Frenchman departs for his military service. As a final fling in the civilian world he drives around with his friends hooting his horn, waving flags and kissing the girls and the day may well end with a meal, several bottles of wine and sometimes a night in the police cells!

France and the Birth of the Common Market

After the Second World War it became clear that Europe could no longer continue to exist in tiny states, but would have to form larger units. Men such as Winston Churchill and Jean Monnet preached the advisability of such AMALGAMATIONS; yet the first nations to merge were neither Britain nor France but Belgium, Netherlands, and Luxemburg, which formed Benelux as early as 1948. If this process continued, it seemed that Europe might form a *bloc* comparable with the two giants of the post-war world, America and Russia. The United Europe Movement scored a success in fact in 1949, when fifteen countries founded the Council of Europe, a sort of international parliament meeting in Strasbourg, France; but by 1953 it was evident that many of these countries were not ready to surrender their political independence.

Map showing the six Common Market countries.

However, in less CONTROVERSIAL sectors advances had already been made; in 1950 the Frenchman, Robert Schuman, proposed the pooling of the coal and steel resources of certain states. In fact, six countries – three already making up Benelux and three more, France, West Germany, and Italy – banded together. The example was followed up in respect of transport, agriculture, health, etc., and there was talk of a customs' union and free trade. Then, as large or small European states lost their former colonies, they turned towards each other and old rivalries disappeared.

It would be a mistake, however, to think that all difficulties were easily overcome. In 1954 the French Lower House of Parliament rejected the notion of a European Defence Community and to this day France prefers to keep her army, navy and air force as much as possible to herself. Moreover, since then France has shown reluctance to rush ahead with the political unification of continental Europe.

In March 1957 an important pact was none the less signed by the 'Six'. According to this Treaty of Rome, there were to be two stages in the development of the Common Market or European Economic Community. The first would break down trade barriers and level off price inequalitites between the Six, whilst creating a European banking system. The second step would involve agriculture and it is on this point that temporarily the E.E.C. lost France and for a time had to manage with five nations round the conference table. However, France managed to iron out her differences, and so what was facetiously referred to as 'Green Europe' came into being.

At one time Great Britain felt that her ties with her Commonwealth should not be weakened by forging a new link with six European nations. But many of these European nations themselves had former colonies, which they managed to satisfy on this issue. Take the example of France herself. She kept the pledge made at Dakar in Africa in December 1959 to grant independence to the African Republics, formerly in her empire; and in May 1960 the Constitution was modified in such a way that the Senate of French *Communauté* was satisfied. By signing agreements with France, henceforth a state could become independent without ceasing to be a member, and an already independent state could join the Community.

Now it turned out that all members of the French Community chose independence and are now members of the United Nations. Four African states left the Community altogether and formed a little group of their own but they nevertheless signed an agreement with the parent country. So, like our own Commonwealth, the French Community consists of equal and independent nations who recognize the President of the Republic, as

President of the Community, just as former British colonies accept Queen Elizabeth II as Head of the Commonwealth.

Member states co-operate in defence, foreign affairs, education, telecommunications, and banking. Economic ties between France and her old colonies have become more important since independence and France grants huge sums of money to aid emergent nations. For instance, between 1959 and 1961 France and the Common Market gave more aid to African countries than either the U.S.A. or Britain did.

In return for this aid, African states associated themselves with the European Common Market. At the end of 1963, eighteen African countries – most of them former French colonies – became associate members of this European organization. This promoted trade between Europe and Africa and proved to be advantageous to both sides. At the same time Europe had preferential treatment in securing raw materials and in having access to vast and expanding African markets; in return France put at the disposal of underdeveloped nations her technical knowledge and inventive genius.

An Ingenious Nation

Three hundred years ago a clever man died prematurely. However, in the course of thirty-nine years he had achieved a few miracles. At the age of twelve, according to his sister Gilberte, this bright boy had discovered the initial propositions of Euclidian geometry *without using a book*! At sixteen he had written an amazingly mature treatise on conical sections; at eighteen he was the inventor of the first practical calculating machine; and yet, despite obvious expertise in mathematics, this brilliant genius, Blaise Pascal, is best known for his religious views. Exceptional, yes; but all the same Pascal was French and the French have always been renowned for their inventive ingenuity. For example, in the following century the joint author of the famous *Encyclopaedia*, D'Alembert, made important discoveries in dynamics. Similarly, differential calculus owes much to Lagrange, who worked with Laplace (1749–1827) in founding the metric system.

In the nineteenth century Leverrier made impressive calculations about

A sensitive short-lived genius, Blaise Pascal.
(*Radio Times Hulton Picture Library*)

55

Cugnot's ungainly automobile runs into trouble.
(Radio Times Hulton Picture Library)

the solar system and found the planet Neptune about the same time as it was discovered by the Englishman, Adams. Henri Poincaré (1854–1912) worked with great success on developing and applying mathematics to mechanics, astronomy and physics.

When we reckon electricity in amps, we are unconsciously paying tribute to the French scientist, Ampère (1775–1836), whose researches led to electro-dynamics and to the telegraph we know today, which was partly developed by another Frenchman, Branly (1884–1940).

In many other fields too, French scientists have distinguished themselves and honoured their nation. As long ago as the sixteenth century, Ambroise Paré taught his students how to LIGATURE arteries. Steam engines owe much to Papin (1647–1714) from Blois.

In 1771 Cugnot produced the first automobile, which may still be seen in the fascinating Conservatoire des Arts et Métiers, the Paris equivalent of the Imperial Science Museum in South Kensington, London.

All budding chemists associate oxygen with Lavoisier (who was guillotined during the French Revolution because of his aristocratic origins), and the laws governing gases with Gay-Lussac (1778–1850). When the

56

doctor comes to sound your chest with his stethoscope, he is indebted to Laënnec (1781–1826) who discovered and perfected this method; and Claude Bernard studying the nervous system, showed the part played by the pancreas. Who would know much about infections and bacilli, without the man who gave his name to a process for STERILIZING milk, Louis Pasteur? Above all, doctors remember Pierre and Marie Curie, who, in the early years of this century, evolved the radium with which we treat cancer. Nor did Frenchmen overlook diseases of the mind. At the Salpêtrière Hospital in Paris, the nineteenth-century psychiatrist, Charcot, studied and treated nervous and psychological disorders.

Turning to another subject altogether, we note that France has always bred outstanding engineers, like de Lesseps, whose name is always linked with the two canals, Suez and Panama. Boring underground, French engineers have helped to make the Mont Blanc Tunnel a splendid piece of co-operation between France and Italy. Seven and a quarter miles long, with a roadway twenty-three feet wide, it is a great help to commerce and tourism and already serious steps are being taken in exploring the sea-bed and approaches to the famous Channel Tunnel, which will be much longer, will involve collaboration between Britain and France and end the age-old physical isolation of our country from the rest of Europe.

Seven and a half miles to Italy, under Mont Blanc. (*Paul Popper*)

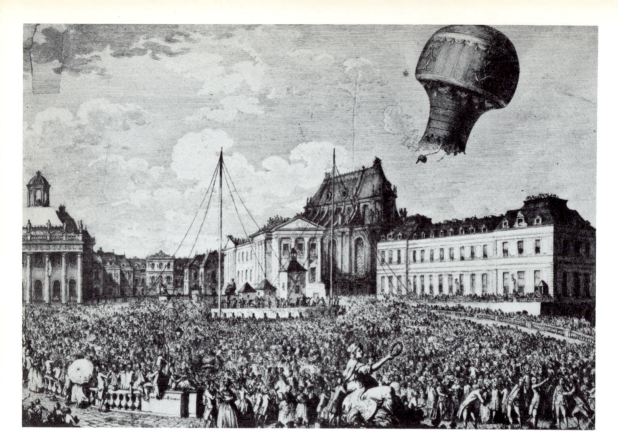

Other clever men have provided France with the Oleron Bridge stretching for a distance of nearly two miles across an arm of the Atlantic, and huge dams like the one at Génissiat in the mountainous Ain Region.

Of these engineering marvels my own particular favourite is the graceful but gigantic suspension bridge across the lower Seine river at Tancarville. Going south you come down a gentle slope, past a monument, and arrive at the toll-booths where, for a car and passengers, you are asked for the equivalent of about twelve shillings. Perhaps it is worth the money after all, for soon you are soaring four hundred feet above the wide river just as though you were seated in a low-flying plane.

In the field of aviation proper, France has known some outstanding pioneers. Montgolfier is a name always associated with the balloon, and indeed the two brothers were making hair-raising ascents in hot-air contraptions at the end of the eighteenth century. In 1785 De Rozier died trying to cross the Channel in just such a precarious device. Luckily for INTREPID aviators, François Blanchard invented the parachute. In 1897

Clément Ader was flying a winged machine and in 1909 Blériot was to be the first airman to cross the Channel.

Photography and cinematography owe much to our French friends. The earliest plates were known as 'daguerrotypes' after Daguerre (1797–1851) and, thanks to this genuis, we have photographs of mid-nineteenth-century personalities. Aptly named, Auguste Lumière and his brother Louis invented cinematography and then perfected colour photography, while Gaumont (1864–1946) made 'talking pictures' possible.

Blind people throughout the world must thank Louis Braille (1809–52) for spending much of his short life making up an alphabet that would allow them to read, for he was blind too. Who would deny in fact, that Braille's invention was one of the greatest of all.

Industrial Modernization

When I was a student in Paris, I was taken along to dine with a man who spent his life carving four-poster beds, replicas of those used by the aristocrats of the seventeenth and eighteenth centuries. If you had seen the results, you would have agreed with me that he was a very great individual craftsman in the true French tradition, which has always encouraged people to work in small groups or quite alone, and to take immense pride in quality.

Unfortunately this idea can hardly survive in an age of mass production and, despite the noble efforts of organizations like the Compagnons du Devoir, which are trying to return in some measure to the ideals of craftsman-guilds, France is streamlining her industry to meet the challenge of the machine age, devoting nearly a quarter of the national income to investment in new factories and industrial processes and providing additional employment for three quarters of a million workers.

Helping with this great effort is the technique of AUTOMATION, used, for instance, at the nationalized glass factory of Saint-Gobain (Chantereine) which turns out sixty-five million square feet of glass a year, the regularity and thickness of each pane being tested by a system using radioactive

Vast amounts of concrete
went into this UNESCO
building in Paris.
(*Keystone Press Agency*)

elements. In metallurgy, building materials, textiles, and chemicals too,
less and less is being left to the operator and more is done and checked
automatically. For instance, in the very north west of the country, near
Dunkirk, the Usinor steel works, supplying some one and a half million
tons of steel a year and expected one day to produce five million, is
thoroughly automated.

So is the Renault car factory near Paris, which makes over 650,000
vehicles a year and exports a quarter of these and therefore has a substantial
share in the two-million export programme of a car industry producing the
following makes of car: Renault, Citroën, Simca, Peugeot and Panhard.
In addition to some of the above, commercial vehicles are supplied by
Saviem-Chausson, Bernard & Berliet. The latter firm is currently providing Paris with its new double-decker buses, though smart Cityrama
coaches full of tourists have long been seen around the Capital.

The building trade offers another excellent example of enterprise and
initiative. France has always led the way in the use of reinforced concrete,
and certain constructions in Britain were undertaken in the nineteen-
thirties by a French company, Mopin. Nowadays French engineers are

busy applying industrial techniques to all aspects of building. Prestressed concrete, developed by Freycinet, has made it possible for the French to make enormous spans for bridges, like Tancarville, whilst saving material at the same time. Another use of this technique was the making of a vast underground water reservoir at the Porte des Lilas in Paris, the capacity being some seven million cubic feet. The great French architect, Le Corbusier, who died in 1965, was one of the first to employ slender columns to support large buildings, and his Swiss hostel in the Cité Universitaire in Paris still attracts visitors; but his most famous concrete monument will always be his housing scheme at Marseilles. Younger men like Jean Prouvé and Marcel Lods have followed his example by applying what is called the 'curtain-wall method' to modern buildings requiring plenty of light and air. The French are also pioneers in the use of glued LAMINATED wood for framing large spaces without any intermediate supports, as in modern churches.

A few years ago I stayed at the Cité Universitaire in Angers and I found that my pleasure at being in that fine city was slightly diminished by just one thing: each morning I was awakened about half past six by the noise of building operations across the road. In July 1967 I visited Angers once more and was quite impressed to discover that all this effort had now borne fruit: the Cité Universitaire, or University precinct consisting of hostels for student accommodation, was now three times as vast as it had been two years before!

Fasten on your headphones for the Cityrama trip with taped commentary!
(*Philip Carr*)

Le Corbusier's famous Swiss House on concrete pillars. (*Philip Carr*)

So speed is one beneficial result of automation and modernization. Another reason for optimism springs from new uses for good craftsmen. Being a truly artistic nation, the French have not forgotten beauty in their new buildings. For example, almost every modern school will proudly show you a tapestry, wood-carving or a mural painting executed by a young artist, who has been very well paid for his services. Thus engineers, architects and artists are involved in a common cause and the balance between the arts and technology has not been neglected.

The last word on this thorny problem concerns my friend of many years ago who, in a tiny workshop at Charenton, carved old-fashioned beds for modern clients. In the midst of this time-consuming process, he had managed to train his dog Jackie to do tricks, one of which involved a slight knowledge of several European languages. Only at *drei*, *trois*, *tre* or *three* would the dog interrupt your counting, throw the sugar lump, neatly balanced on his nose, in the air and devour it. A stupid waste of time in the twentieth century of machines and computers? I think not: after all, the art of living is to find time for the little things.

Sources of Power

France was the first nation to make a significant use of the tides to create electricity. Across the mouth of the Breton River Rance there is now a tremendous concrete dam trapping the energy of four tides a day. In addition to this wonderful scheme, France is pushing ahead with the development of a much older source of supply – hydroelectric power, amusingly known as *houille blanche* ('white coal'). Dams like Génissiat or Tignes trap behind a concrete barrier the waters of French rivers and mountain torrents. Massive dynamos spin into life, generating current for the national grid. At peak hours, some of this electricity comes our way through a cable laid beneath the Channel, for happily our rush hours and the French rush hours do not quite coincide. But power-hungry Europe continues to increase demand and, in late July 1967, yet another hydro-electric station was opened at Pierre-Bénite on the Rhône – this time with the additional benefit of enabling canal shipping to pass into that river.

This is a very important facility in the case of a country that stands at the crossroads of Europe. But, of all forms of internal transport, road haulage rules supreme and requires oil and petrol. That is why Algerian oil has been made to flow through pipes under the Mediterranean Sea; but that is by no means the end of the affair. From there a giant south-European pipeline leads to eastern France and the German Ruhr which makes equally heavy demands for power. This pipe connects the oil port near Marseilles with Neustadt in Germany and passes via Lyons, Besançon, Belfort, Strasbourg and across the frontier.

Also from the Etang de Berre, near Marseilles, there will be a pipeline for finished products that will span eastern France and supply places like Geneva airport in Switzerland with petrol. It will be 525 miles long and carry millions of tons of fuel. And the French think they have found an answer to the fire hazard. The *Prométhée* is fire-extinguishing equipment using bicarbonate of soda, which has already proved capable of putting out a flame as high as a building.

In the south west lies France's new power house of natural gas, Lacq, discovered in 1949. Pipelines have been laid from this area to many parts of the Republic, whilst Lacq also produces important by-products like sulphur, fertilizers, chemicals and metals.

Of course, the most up-to-date source of power is the atom and indeed France has several nuclear power stations feeding the national grid, so that she now ranks fourth in this field and employs some thirty thousand workers in this industry. At Cadarache travellers notice the outlines of an experimental pile and reactors have already been installed there, as well as at Fontenay-aux-Roses, Marcoule, Pierrelatte, Saclay and Grenoble. A factory at Forez is also producing uranium in such quantities that France has already become western Europe's leading supplier. She also has an agreement for drawing supplies from the African Republic of Niger, where huge deposits exist. At Saint-Laurent-des-Eaux on the Loire, a large atomic power station has changed the landscape of this part of the famous valley, especially as the possibility of flooding has obliged the engineers to raise the construction upon a high platform of earth. This new plant will produce electricity in commercially economic quantities – three million kilowatts to be precise. At the end of 1966 it was announced that an exact copy of the Saint-Laurent nuclear power station had been sold to Spain. This will be jointly useful, since Spain too is an important source of uranium. Not far from Saint-Laurent, at Chinon, there is a huge nuclear power station with three reactors using natural uranium and designed to produce enormous amounts of power.

By applying this industrial progress to her navy, France is now able to build nuclear submarines. As a preliminary test, at the Cadarache Research Centre scientists imagined that a ship went round the world – without leaving the test bench of course – 'sailing' from Brest in October 1965. As early as 1960 all this had been planned. The land prototype or model of the nuclear reactor needed to propel such a submarine had become 'critical' (active) in August 1964, and soon the reactor was supplying the power necessary to operate such a vehicle. But submarines need enriched uranium and this poses the problem of crew safety. Despite this difficulty, the experimental submarine *Gymnote* continued to study the effects of pitching and rolling on the new types of vessel and in March 1967 France's first nuclear submarine, *Le Redoutable*, slid down the slipway into the sea. The second known as *Le Terrible*, will also be very aptly named, as these war vessels should strike fear into the hearts of any enemy—if one were foolish enough to engage in war against a country which now possesses an effective hydrogen bomb.

Opposite: The power-station
at Saint-Laurent-des-Eaux on
the river Loire, near Orléans.
(*Brigaud Photothèque EDC*)

The Space Programme

France has virtually decided to be independent in space research, a decision which has strained her resources in many ways and led to herculean efforts on her part.

The last months of 1965 saw an intensification of these efforts. The Ministry of the Armed Forces announced, for instance, that a *Saphir* rocket, consisting of the first two stages of the future *Diamant* rocket, had been launched from a site in Algeria. It soared up to 722 miles and was regarded as a complete success. This was one of the final trials before the real thing. Early in 1966 the *Diamant* sent into orbit a research satellite and in 1969 a *Super-Diamant* rocket is to launch satellites from Guiana. The first *Diamant* rocket was a three-stage launcher consisting of an *Emeraude* rocket, a *Topaze* rocket and a *Rubis* rocket. From this you can see that the French are using the jewellers' vocabulary to distinguish one space vehicle from another!

Although she intends to discourage foreign influence, France has not been too proud to allow American or Russian space organizations to launch satellites for her, and some distinguished French scientists persuaded the Gemini team to perform experiments for them during flight. French firms are also involved in production of the international *Intelsat IV* and two other satellites in the *Symphony* range.

The space programme has been well prepared and, with the exception of small setbacks, so far carried out successfully by the C.N.E.S. – that is, the National Centre for Space Studies. The C.N.E.S. has also encouraged Space Clubs for young people; the result is that, from four in 1963, there were forty in 1967. Under professional supervision these enthusiasts build a rocket head, and, between 1963 and 1967, forty rockets were launched for clubs by the C.N.E.S.

This organization planned the launching site in Guiana to replace the one in North Africa. Since the new one is closer to the Equator, it allows rockets to be launched across the poles, if desired. So France is relying upon her former colonies: just as French Polynesia is used for atomic testing, so Guiana is available for space experiments. In the military sphere, France plans to defend herself on all sides, and by 1970 will have, deployed and ready, twenty-seven ballistic missiles of 2,000 miles range.

The French claim that technical progress has given a new stimulus to certain industries. For example, the manufacture of glass fibre, which is

Diagram of the *'Diamant'* satellite launcher. (The length and diameter are shown in millimetres.)

66

The Sahara testing ground for
rockets and satellites.
(*United Press International*)

needed in space efforts, has increased very considerably in recent months.
Moreover many thousands of people are employed in new ventures, for
Germany, India, Spain, and the Argentine have ordered French rockets.
By using her satellites France expects to improve telecommunications and
television services and provide a direct telephone and television link with
all the countries of her former colonial empire in Africa, the Overseas
Departments, the West Indies, Guiana, etc. Sea and air navigation also
profit from these modern marvels, and farmers may benefit from improved
weather forecasting.

Communications

Before the Second World War they used to tell a tale about the funny little railway line that began in a 'bay' at Enghien station, near Paris and ended up the hill at Montmorency, three stations in all. The train was the most amusing affair with two-tier carriages of an obsolete design, which the ancient engine pushed up hill and then pulled back again. Yet, despite its age and modest appointments, this queer little train had three classes of passengers – third class was on the 'upper deck'. To our story, then; one day the train broke down as usual and found itself quite unable to propel the carriages up the hill. So the order went around: first-class passengers stay where they are; second-class passengers get out and walk and third class passengers get out and push. In the midst of these bewildering and exhausting manoeuvres, along came a ticket inspector, who asked to see the tickets of the poor travellers, perspiring freely as they heaved away at the rear buffers. Grimly he surveyed the piece of card offered by a little man who was puffing and blowing as he toiled away in his shirt sleeves. 'Sorry, sir, but I shall have to fine you' said the official. 'Why?', asked the little man. 'Because you have only a third-class ticket and you are pushing a second-class carriage!'

Well, the French, who can make fun of anything, certainly found their railways humorous in those days. Since the war, however, all that has changed and with reason. In 1945 many bridges, railways and roads were either totally destroyed or damaged beyond repair. However, as is so often the case when a country is down-and-out, the national will to make a better future was strong and on the railways in particular miracles of reconstruction and modernization were performed. Progress is still incredibly rapid. In 1953 two-thirds of trains were pulled by steam locomotives, and diesel traction was almost non-existent. By 1966 electric engines were pulling three-quarters of all trains and diesel engines had crept up to second place. In the south west of France, near Bordeaux, an electric train has travelled at 331 kilometres an hour, which is the world record.

Jean Bertin, a French engineer, thinks he has found a solution to the traffic problem in the *aerotrain*. This is a wingless vehicle, able to carry passengers at speeds of two to three hundred miles per hour, so that towns at present too far apart for daily travel will now be reached in the time we take to go home by bus or underground. France has already invested three

68

million francs in M. Bertin's *aerotrain*, which is driven by propellers like an aeroplane. It travels on a concrete platform with a wall in the centre acting as a guide rail. When it sets off, the *aerotrain* is lifted from the ground by jets of air striking the platform, whilst other jets are directed against the wall to prevent any actual contact between train and cement. The result is that the vehicle floats along without friction, transporting in speed and

Bertin's *aerotrain* runs on a cushion of air like a hover-craft.
(United Press International)

69

The Concorde raises an important question: can we tolerate the sonic boom?
(*Keystone Press Agency*)

The Franco-British Jaguar is rolled out.
(*Keystone Press Agency*)

comfort a hundred passengers in each carriage. The first aerotrain route will carry students between Orléans University and the centre of that city and later run on to Paris too.

All this sounds like a chapter from Jules Verne come true. However, in the development of ordinary roads, the French have less to show than many other European countries. Unfortunately their *autoroutes* are still rare but, with so many cars on the road, the building programme must be intensified. All this construction costs a great deal of money. Some of the new highways involve heavy tolls, therefore. For instance, half the journey from Calais to Nice can be made on *autoroutes*, but at the cost of about three pounds and soon, with more toll roads coming into use, that charge is expected to rise to about the equivalent of five pounds.

Railways and roads have not been the only form of communication to interest the French in recent years. Consider, for instance, the helicopters which, leaving the Invalides terminal, roar over Paris on their way to Orly airport or to the Paris heliport on the Boulevard Périphérique. Turn, then, to ordinary planes. The jet-propelled Caravelle aircraft has been used and sold widely in the world, and many countries have copied the French in locating the engines in the rear. Anglo-French projects are of particular interest to us. Apart from the Concorde supersonic airliner – which is expected to fly the Atlantic at fifteen hundred miles per hour in under three hours – there are the Eurobus idea in collaboration with West Germany, helicopters and several versions of the Jaguar supersonic strike military 'plane for the French Air Force and our own. On January 8, 1968 the French Minister for the Armed Forces travelled to London to sign the Jaguar agreement with our own Minister of Defence. So Britain and France stand side by side in charting an exciting future in the skies.

Sea Transport

Atlantic liners may seem traditional compared with planes. Yet the 1,025 feet *France*, the longest ship in the world, is designed to carry 2,1000 passengers at thirty-one knots. It has proved its popularity, for not all travellers want to reach New York in three hours. Many think it better and safer to take about five days in the luxury of the greatest of the French ships! Recently I found myself in Le Havre when *France* was due to arrive from

the U.S.A. Not a room was to be had in any of the hotels, since many friends and relations had come to meet the vessel's passengers and take them by car to Paris. When, in mid-afternoon on a hot summer's day, the liner was sighted out at sea, a distinct buzz of excitement went round the busy port and the crowded beach. By the time I had reached the Porte Océane, near the entrance to the harbour, there she was, her funnels resembling a spaniel's ears with their curious flaps. How quickly she finally slipped into port behind the apparently diminutive tugboat! This immense ship, which the French received as war reparation from the Germans, had reached home safely once more.

Whereas the liner *France* pays tribute to its country, other ships often bear the names of distinguished men from the past. In order to chart and study the seas of the world, France launched the *Jean-Charcot*, which claims to be very noiseless and manoeuvreable and, in order to transport gas by refrigerated methods, a vessel called the *Jules Verne*. This ship carries twenty-five thousand cubic metres of methane gas at a speed of seventeen knots: the gas which evaporates slowly in the course of the voyage is actually used to propel the ship itself, which has a jet turbine unit developing fifteen thousand horse power. At fifty million francs, it is considered to be a bargain and a wonderful companion for the already operating *Pythagore*, which performs similar duties. In general, we can also say that, whereas many other countries are losing their tonnage, France expanded her merchant navy by a quarter of a million tons between 1966 and 1967.

At the other end of the nautical scale, France is working out a minor miracle for her tiniest transport ships, canal barges. Now, anyone knows that barges climb hills by means of locks, but these take time. For example, on the Rhine-Marne canal in the north east there are seventeen locks in the Zorn Valley alone – a distance of two miles or so – and this means a delay of ten to twelve hours. Or rather, it *did*: by 1967 the same distance could be covered in forty minutes! Barges now climb hills pushed by a sort of bulldozer propelling the water rather than the barge itself.

But, however modernized, barges cannot compete with really modern craft. Consider, for instance, another idea worked out by Monsieur Bertin, the *naviplane*. Like a hovercraft, this consists of an aeroglider capable of carrying up to five hundred men or thirty vehicles at about a hundred miles per hour across stretches of sea or inland waterway. Clever French engineers are also experimenting with a *telescaph*. This is made up of a chain of cabins resembling air bubbles, towed through the water like a sea-borne train. Since July 1967, it has been possible to try the new *telescaph* service at Marseilles. The public can now spend seventy-five minutes viewing marine life twenty-four feet below the surface!

Opposite: The new method of taking a dip – by *telescaph* !
(*United Press International*)

73

The Press

Let us turn, then, to a different form of communication. Frenchmen are very fond of their newspapers and magazines, a fact which is proved by the considerable number sold. There are about fifteen thousand different publications of this sort, the total circulation per issue amounting to one hundred and forty million copies! Daily papers alone sell about twelve million copies, and it has been estimated that every day any given group of a hundred French people purchase twenty-four dailies.

Look at Paris first. Here there are thirteen political and news dailies, nine appearing in the morning, four in the evening and five specialized journals (i.e. concerned with things like finance and racing) coming on to the bookstalls each day too. This accounts for four million copies. With a circulation of one and a quarter million, *France-Soir* (which appears in different editions at many hours of the day) tops the list. With three-quarters of a million copies on sale in the kiosks, *Le Parisien Libéré*, which deals with Parisian, as well as general news, comes second, followed closely by the half million copies of *Le Figaro*, a right-wing or Conservative paper containing a social diary and articles contributed by important writers like Pierre Gaxotte the historian, and Jacques de Lacretelle the novelist.

The tradespeople of the capital naturally choose a paper catering for their own needs, and this they find in *L'Aurore*, with its ample coverage of business and finance and with a circulation of the same order as *Le Figaro*. Just over half this circulation is achieved by *Paris-Jour*, which is smaller in size and appeals to younger readers of both sexes. Learned researchers leaving the Bibliothèque Nationale find themselves faced with a vendor of a much more serious paper devoid of illustrations, but crammed with facts and called *Le Monde*. It affords some proof that Paris is one of the great intellectual centres of the world, for it sells some quarter of a million copies per day.

Passing on to more specialized organs of the Parisian press, we find one which is cried around the streets on Sunday mornings by obviously sincere amateur sellers, *L'Humanité* the official organ of the large Communist Party. This runs to some two hundred thousand copies and, with *Les Echos*, is one of the few successful party newspapers. At the other extreme lies *La Croix*, which, as the name suggests, appeals to Catholics but offers in addition a good deal of economic and social discussion.

We must not, however, overlook the hundred or so dailies that appear

Opposite: Titles of some of the principal Paris dailies. (*Service de Presse, The French Embassy*)

outside Paris and sell seven and a half million copies. Almost all of these are on the bookstalls in the morning, since only the biggest towns manage to print an evening paper. The largest regional paper is *Ouest-France*, based on Rennes in Brittany, then *Le Progrès* (Lyons), *La Voix du Nord* (Lille) and in the south *La Dépêche du Midi* is widely read.

Of the weeklies, perhaps the most influential is the humorous *Canard Enchaîné*. Now *canard* means either 'hoax' or 'rag' and this newspaper pokes fun at national figures like the President. It sells over three hundred thousand copies and its regular features often appear later in book form. *France-Dimanche* and *Ici Paris* specialize, on the other hand, in revealing the secrets of the stars and of world society. On the serious side, the left-wing *Express* sells about two hundred thousand each week, but literary magazines like *Les Nouvelles Littéraires* and *Le Figaro Littéraire* do well also. For those who are interested in potted history with suitable illustrations, there are *Miroir de l'Histoire* and *Historia*. Readers anxious to find out what is on in town or on television have only to buy *La Semaine de Paris*, *Vingt-Quatre Heures*, or consult *Paris Presse's* TV column or the magazine *Télé-Sept-Jours*, to discover the items they require.

One impressive feature about the reading habits of the French is demonstrated by their love of periodicals and magazines. This arises partly from the fact that an agricultural country constantly seeks information about urban habits and particularly about fashion and dress; partly too from the national desire to keep abreast by reading as much as possible. This desire is difficult to satisfy, for France has very few lending libraries.

The result of this is obvious. Take for instance the case of the *Echo des Françaises*, sold only by subscription and yet finding its way into one and three quarter million homes; or the more renowned *Paris-Match*, which, despite all that television can do, is selling some one and a half million copies! In fact, *Paris-Match* is PHENOMENAL in a host of different ways too. It acquired the first European rights to American space pictures; it has at least fifty reporters and thirty photographers, most of whom have worked with this team since the first issue; in pounds, its annual turnover amounts to twelve million with a profit of £350,000; in Britain it has doubled its sale in five years. Some considerable way behind this outstanding magazine come the French version of *Readers' Digest* and *France-Dimanche*, which everyone seems to read at the week-end. To keep abreast of fashion French women buy *Marie-Claire* and *La Maison de Marie-Claire* too.

All in all, then, our French friends are avid readers of the daily and weekly press.

Johnny Halliday and Sylvie Vartan, husband and wife, are both singers.
(*Paul Popper*)

Teenage Magazines

'C'est un tube terrible, le pantalon C.', announces a bold trouser advertisement in *Salut les Copains*, which lies open on my desk as I write. But, in case any young linguist imagines that this means what it appears to mean, let me quickly reassure him that the advertisement, illustrated by the smartest modern garment he has ever seen, is by no means intended to suggest that the trousers in question are either too tight or are horrible to contemplate, for in French teenage talk, *tube* means 'a hit' and *terrible* means 'smashing' or 'terrific'; and there you have it: a whole new language invented by young people, the *copains* or 'pals' who frequent *discothèques* and clubs which they refer to as *la loco*. To them everything must be *dans le vent* ('with it'), and magazines cater for this. Unfortunately such magazines tend to encourage what Professor Etiemble of Paris calls *le franglais*, a nasty mixture of two languages, harmful to both. For instance, the word *polo*, borrowed from our own word for a high-necked sweater, means a different kind of garment in French!

The number of *Salut les Copains* before me has a photograph of our own Beatles on the cover. Inside there are articles and pictures of the stars,

Françoise Hardy records chiefly her own songs and accompanies herself on the guitar.
(*Paul Popper*)

Frank Alamo, Adamo, Claude François, Françoise Hardy, Sylvie Vartan, Johnny Halliday, as well as British and American pop idols. Happily a thoughtful editor provides his reader with the first three sections (A–C) of a new illustrated dictionary to help us to understand the rest. Some words we can guess, of course. For instance the word for 'pop', *yé-yé*, is derived from 'Yeah! Yeah!' VOCIFERATED by our own singers. President de Gaulle once listened to Johnny Halliday and decided that the noise resembled that of an army band, and this too was noted.

Salut les Copains sells over a million copies each time it appears. The advertisements, as we have already seen, are quite fascinating. It is easy to conclude that French teenagers desire huge muscles and detest spots and pimples; that they would all love to play the guitar without too much

78

effort; that they favour inscribed tee-shirts and ties and eat sweets; that they have a *hit parade* (they use the same word) and follow the fortunes of their favourite week by week; and that girls in particular like new shoes and horoscopes.

Anything with an English title appeals to them. Also on my desk is a copy of *Top*, which, unlike *Salut*, can be stuffed into the pocket to read in the bus or underground. On the cover of this small magazine is Michael Caine, looking very sinister indeed and described as one of the 'successeurs de James Bond'. Items about Hollywood, about the theatre and the cinema rub shoulders with articles devoted to sport of all kinds, to dress, to the latest novels and even to history, whilst our 'roving reporter' sends in news from a different foreign country each week. Needless to say, record reviews play a big part in *Top*, which also takes a serious look at technical marvels of our time and at interesting holiday haunts. Add to this a dash of humour in the form of cartoons and jokes, a crossword puzzle, a short story and an advertisement for a key ring containing a 'real' book in miniature and you can see that the teenagers across the Channel are well supplied.

Radio, Television and Postal Services

Any visitor to the French capital will have noticed, on the Passy bank of the Seine opposite the Eiffel Tower, a very large modern building with a circular form and a central tower. This is the Maison de la Radio, the national radio centre. (Most television is located elsewhere at present.) The offices are on the outside ring, the inner ring consists of studios and concert halls, whilst the central tower contains storage facilities and archives.

The State service is called ORTF, or *Office de Radiodiffusion et de Télévision Française*. It deals with three radio and two television networks. The Saar in southern Germany (Europe No. 1), Monte Carlo and Luxemburg offer facilities to advertisers, whose programmes are beamed towards France and are said to attract more listeners than the national stations.

Sales of receiving sets in recent years have been amazing. Whereas in late 1949 there were six and a half million radios in use in France, the

79

Europe's largest circular building – the Paris Radio Centre.
(*French Government Tourist Office*)

transistor craze has now added another ten million to this estimated total and enabled younger French citizens to keep up with events. Besides these sixteen million radio receivers, there are nearly eight million television sets – about half as many as in England. The consequence of these developments is that eighty-five per cent of homes have radio and forty per cent television.

At the same time, France is offering the world the SECAM system of colour TV, appropriately invented by Henri de France, thanks to whose genius and skill huge masts are beginning to spring up all over France. Whilst many accuse television of disrupting family life and encouraging sex and violence, the creation of *télé-clubs* in RURAL areas has had beneficial social consequences. The part played by radio and television in forming public taste is something of which the French are very conscious, and in particular the 'wireless' supplies culture and music of a high order, sometimes at the risk of boring the public. Indeed, British visitors to France are often immediately aware that much of French radio and television resembles their own Third or Music programmes – for instance, the French Music Programme and France-Culture, of which the planners at ORTF are inordinately proud. On the whole France's radio directors are enlightened patrons of the arts. A visitor to the radio centre in Paris will find murals by men like Jean Cocteau, Stalhy, Mathieu and Bazaine, and very modern decor throughout the building, which, with a surface area of ten acres, is the largest circular construction in Europe, and a headquarters worthy of a nation anxious to keep abreast of developments and perhaps to lead the world in some things.

Another illustration of this is the French Post Office or PTT (*Postes, Télégrammes et Téléphones*), modernized in the past twenty years. We may have laughed in our time at the postman in the film, *Jour de Fête*, suddenly goaded into frenzied 'efficiency' by a dramatic short film about American methods, but nowadays the joke would tend to lose its point.

The French Post Office is increasingly automated; machines are used to sort letters and parcels, issue money-orders and deal with banking services.

The Film Industry

A couple of years ago climbing the steep and narrow streets of the Montmartre hill in Paris, I came upon a scene which made me grab my camera. Here before my very eyes were a typical nursemaid with a high pram, a man in a blue smock sweeping the gutter, a fat boy in his sailor suit and a very Parisian policeman. Hastily I took the picture, which turned out

Film-making: Actors enjoy a studio joke before being 'hanged'.
(Paul Popper)

Jean-Luc Godard.
(*Paul Popper*)

well; but I cannot use it to demonstrate a Paris street, because, immediately after I had pressed the shutter-release, I noticed under the trees a camera team with impressive apparatus and a large reflector to light up the darker side of the scene. For the thousandth time, it would seem, I had come upon a film crew in the streets of Paris; the typically French people were being paid, for they were professional actors!

There can be no doubt that France was a pioneer of films, for Daguerre, Niepce, Marey, Reynaud and others are well-known. It was in 1895 that the Lumière brothers, who had invented the motion-picture camera, held the world's first public film show in Paris: in the following year, 1896, Georges Méliès perfected motion-picture techniques and somewhat later Emile Cohl created the first cartoon films. Another name always associated with cinema is that of Charles Pathé.

Since the end of the Second World War, France has had a busy film industry. Before 1958, it was sustained by pre-war directors like Duvivier, Carné, and René Clair, and some older men like Cocteau and Renoir came back with vigour. Other film-makers emerged as a direct result of the war – men like Clément and Becker, for instance. There was also a reaction against the idea of making the film dependent upon a book.

What is now known as the 'New Wave' (*Nouvelle Vague*) was brought into being by artists like Astruc, Melville and Vadim, who looked ahead to less conventional and more adventurous geniuses like Jean-Luc Godard, who, with Chabrol, Truffaut and Resnais, began to make his name between 1957 and 1958. A very interesting place in modern cinema is occupied by the novelist Alain Robbe-Grillet, whose films are very strange indeed. A few months ago I had the pleasure of talking to Monsieur Robbe-Grillet and was surprised by the revelation that he had been trained as an engineer. Yet on second thoughts a knowledge of the working and construction of things should help. For instance, it was a Frenchman called Chrétien who invented the process by which pictures can be compressed during filming and then enlarged during projecting thus permitting the development of such marvels as cinemascope.

As long ago as 1946 France acquired a Centre National de la Cinématographie, under the authority of the Minister of State for Cultural Affairs which supervises the administrative and financial side of the effort. The head of this Centre is in charge of employment, working schedules and modernization of studios. He grants loans and subsidies to producers, issues work cards and permits, and keeps records of contracts and films. In 1966, ninety-five films were made by France alone and another thirty-five in collaboration with other nations.

Since 1945 cinema clubs have sprung up all over France. No longer are they the monopoly of intellectuals and we find the man-in-the-street staying behind after the show to discuss the films. Cinema-going has been maintained rather better than in other countries, for France has still some five thousand cinemas. Under the impact of television, attendances have declined, of course, though, in 1966, 232 million tickets were still sold at box-offices. In any case, instead of judging entirely by the commercial rewards arising from receipts at the box-office, the French have a system of bonuses, which they pay to those who make shorter films of high quality – the most important criterion in France. If only Hollywood had paid more attention to such matters, she would be remembered with more affection by generations of cinema-goers.

Sport

At one time France's national sport was undoubtedly cycling, which is still followed very enthusiastically, especially in the north. In this sport France secured four gold medals in the 1968 Olympics. And who could possibly overlook the Tour de France? When I arrive in Paris each summer, I notice that my taxi-driver is concentrating more on his transistor than on the road and is really wondering whether some ace like Poulidor or Anquetil is going win the *maillot jaune* – the yellow tee-shirt – symbolizing success in the current day's stage (*étape*) of the long race. I also know that, when he has finally deposited me and my baggage, he will hasten to the nearest café to watch on the TV screen the *peloton* of cyclists, closely pursued by a circus of pressmen, promoters, radio vans, cycle-manufacturers' spares' wagons and the like. All round the perimeter of the Republic they go, over wet roads, in blistering heat, through dangerous mountain passes, past the rocky coves of Brittany and along the dazzling Cote d'Azur – all the way to the Parc des Princes stadium in Paris, where they must ride a few final laps to entertain and thrill the Bastille-Day crowd on July 14.

Some traditional sports are less commercialized than cycling. Frenchmen of all classes hunt and shoot. Nearly two million of them have shooting licences, compared with 380,000 here; since the French Revolution it has become a jealously guarded right. However, for those who prefer more sedate sport, nothing compares with the national craze for fishing. I remember gazing in amused disbelief at a one-legged French worker in the port of Dunkirk, who solemnly backed his Citroen 2 CV motor-car up to the quayside, affixed to the rear a kind of crane, to which he then attached a winch

The Tour de France passes through the mountains.
(Keystone Press Agency)

and a square *carrelet*. When this net was retrieved from the depths of Dunkirk harbour, it was full of fish; then the operation recommenced! Every river has its fanatics; even the Seine in the middle of the City of Paris is lined with men in blue overalls and berets watching and hoping, and occasionally catching gudgeon. Not content with this, some more adventurous types stake their little cobble boats – precisely the same pattern used by the Romans when they occupied Paris – in the centre of the stream and sit there motionless until the next picnic meal. Moreover, the fish that the British would throw back, the French *sportif* will take home for his supper! 'Waste not, want not' tends to be France's maxim!

It is true, however, that, in a changing world, new pastimes are replacing older ones. Today France's main sport is football – who can forget Kopa and Fontaine? – whilst ski-ing comes close behind in the popularity stakes.

Boules can be played almost anywhere.
(Keystone Press Agency)

American imports like basket-ball, British sports like rugby, vie for favour with traditional obsessions like *boules* (or *pétanque* in the south), which is like bowls in some ways, but unlike our own game in that you are allowed to bombard your opponent's forces and do not need a bowling green. Add to this list tennis, judo, athletics, sailing, climbing, swimming, table-tennis, and volley-ball and you will understand why there is such a multiplicity of organizations catering for the many sports practised in the Republic, especially on Sundays.

Today France claims to have sixty-six thousand sports clubs with three million members. Federations like the Union des Centres de Plein Air link them together and deal on their behalf with the State. They also organize competitions and settle the rules. Finally there is a national committee to group the federations together. This *Haut Comité des Sports* advises the government on policy and is presided over by the Prime Minister. The State supplies considerable sums of money to sporting organizations: four times as much in 1965 as in 1958 – some measure of the national concern with sporting prowess. And by the end of 1965, the first programme carried through with government aid had provided France with a thousand sports grounds, six hundred swimming baths and one thousand gymnasia. Today the demand is met in Paris by a new stadium accommodating some hundred thousand sports-fans and two new sports grounds, one to the east and the other to the south west of the capital.

A recent opinion poll revealed that young people are requesting more games and physical activity than ever before, and this is reflected in many ways. For instance, between 1961 and 1963 the training-rate of instructors and regional coaches doubled. The result of all this effort, which is certainly tied up with a new faith in the future and the national recovery of self-respect, is to be seen on all sides. Think of runners like Michel Jazy and Colette Besson – a gold medallist at the 1968 Olympics in Mexico, swimmers like Christine Caron or Alain Mosconi, skiers like the Goitschel, Guy Périllat, Annie Famose, and above all Jean-Claude Killy, winner of three gold medals in the 1968 Winter Olympics at Grenoble, and you will readily understand why the French have won nearly four hundred medals in Olympic games since 1896. The fact that they have done so much better in *recent* contests of this sort is easily explained. Competitors in the '68 Winter Olympics were given eight months leave of absence from work and, to assist training, were provided with six full-time masseurs, fifty soldiers to tend their ski-runs and even a private plane to take them quickly to their *pistes* (runs): and, on the Games themselves, the Republic spent about two hundred million pounds. Vive le Sport!

Culture and Literature

Caen's Cultural Centre.
(*French Government Tourist Office*)

Despite her sporting instincts France has not forgotten that within her frontiers have lived some of the greatest in the world of art and culture. The Fifth Republic possesses a Ministry of Cultural Affairs which, while making available to the masses the best in art and literature, is ever conscious that it has behind it a long tradition of protection and patronage. For example, the French Academy was founded by Louis XIII and Cardinal Richelieu; the Bibliothèque Nationale's vast collection of books was started by Louis XIV, who also founded the Comédie Française and the Academy of Science; the Musée des Arts Décoratifs was inaugurated by Louis XV; and so on.

The present Ministry controls and encourages theatres, music, and cultural centres. Progress proceeds with great speed. Caen, for instance, has a wonderful cultural centre with a very up-to-date theatre. Le Havre possesses its Musée de la Maison de la Culture – a sort of pilot scheme for a wider national extension of such facilities, providing a place where lectures, films, concerts and plays can follow close on the heels of exhibitions held during the day. For there are movable partitions in this building, so that rooms can be changed around at a moment's notice to accommodate new events. Even more striking is the cultural centre at Grenoble, for here,

87

instead of the fairly modern revolving stage, the ingenious French have installed a revolving auditorium to effect changes of scene!

Bourges and Ménilmontant (a Paris suburb) have recently acquired cultural centres, whilst Amiens refers to hers as a 'factory of leisure'. Inside, you will find two theatres, and two lecture-exhibition halls arranged around a wide, central stair.

But no theatre would exist without the dramatist; and it is clear that culture cannot survive without a good supply of literary works. In this domain our French friends are particularly active and successful. It is not by chance that in the past twenty years no less than five French men have gained the coveted Nobel Prize for literature. On the national front too, in addition to awards made by foundations like the Académie Goncourt and the French Academy itself (which disposes of about seventy such prizes each year), the government offers a *Grand Prix National des Lettres*.

Since this affords ample evidence of an exceptional interest in the writing of books, we may well ask ourselves what special characteristics differentiate the literary French from other nationals. Putting the answer very succinctly, we may say that they are concerned above all with the characteristics that distinguish man from all other created beings, which means principally the soul, the mind and ideas. So, until industrial civilization made it strictly necessary for people to specialize and particularly to learn the technical aspects of life, Frenchmen resisted limitations upon their ideas. They preferred to talk in general terms in the salons, in parliament, in their academies, in the press and in the cafés.

This tendency is quite apparent in French literature, which was created above all for the *honnête homme*, that is, for the average, decent citizen of good intentions and of cultural aspirations. Already in the sixteenth century, the period sometimes called the RENAISSANCE, writers were beginning to address themselves to the *honnête homme*; but it was the seventeenth century, the *Grand Siècle* or Great Century, which really began to cater for this decent fellow, this ideal man who had no desire at all to specialize, but was very anxious to be furnished with general ideas. However, we have seen that general ideas cannot be discussed unless we consider man himself, so writers tended to be what we now call psychologists, concerned with what goes on inside our minds and hearts, with our thoughts, reactions and feelings.

Just as the great essayist, Montaigne, revealed in the sixteenth century this tendency to look within and at the same time to disclose ideas of universal value and truth, so in the seventeenth century Descartes, finding himself shut up all alone in a *poêle*, or heated room, during a terrible winter in Holland, thought out a new approach to the science of philosophy, that is to the study of existence and of ideas.

The theatre too displayed the same characteristics. Jean Racine brought dramatic writing to the highest peak in the *Grand Siècle* by concentrating the action of his plays. Very few characters on the stage, little or no movement or physical action, actors forced to use their hands, and particularly their eyes, more than any other part of the body; the whole interest centred, not in war or ambition, but in men and women and how they behave and react to each other, especially when love is involved – that is the world of Racine. Once again, it is directed towards man's heart and soul and proves again French preoccupation with the mind and with ideas of general value and interest.

The eighteenth century tended to stress natural science, but without losing its interest in man. Montesquieu was concerned with man in society, with his laws and customs; Voltaire with man's religion and intellect; Rousseau with man's heart and soul and his form of government.

The nineteenth century was especially the century of gifted novelists and poets and here again the French showed their dominant interest in the heart and mind. Balzac, Stendhal, Hugo, Flaubert wrote novels about the way men and women feel and act, but they were in fact analysing man in

The Comédie Française attached to the Palais-Royal.
(French Government Tourist Office)

general. Poets like Baudelaire, Rimbaud, Verlaine or Mallarmé composed lines of verse that ring true for all who read them, because they are written by men who cared about every man and looked within their own consciousness to find him. Humanity on parade – that is the literature of the French nineteenth century.

And what of our own twentieth century? The same features are apparent here too. Jean-Paul Sartre tells his readers that *existentialism*, the type of philosophy which he helped to popularize after the Second World War, is a 'humanism'. By way of proof, he goes on to assert that he is studying first man's independent existence, apart from all ideas of God and therefore man's right to make what he will of his own life for which he is responsible. The snag is, of course, that man does not exist all alone. Difficulties arise for him because he has to live with other people, for whom he is also responsible since they too are human beings. Other existentialists, whilst not agreeing completely with Sartre, have similar attitudes. The point is that, like almost every French writer since the beginning of literature, they are writing about what goes on inside each one of us and how we live one with another.

French Painting

Many of the characteristics, trends and fancies of the great schools of literature were represented in French art too. This is because the French have always been renowned for their love of painting and sculpture and because, above all places, Paris is pre-eminently the capital of art.

Nevertheless, we begin our review of French painting in the south of France. In the fifteenth century Provence nurtured the French Primitives, foremost among whom were Fouquet and the anonymous 'Maître de Moulins'. These early artists showed the influence of the Flemish schools, and, in the second case, of Italian models too.

As the harshness of northern styles was softened by southern refinement, RENAISSANCE monarchs, in pursuit of fine living, invited Italians like Andrea del Sarto and Leonardo da Vinci to design and decorate their palaces. In one such palace the School of Fontainebleau was established, and painters like Clouet with skill and daintiness depicted ladies of the court.

Many and varied were the styles of the seventeenth century. Under Louis XIII, Vouet continued to uphold the ideals of the Fontainebleau

School; but at the same time Le Sueur was turning his attention to the sincere portrayal of religious themes and the Le Nain brothers were showing the world what peasant life was really like. Another such Naturalist, Philippe de Champaigne, managed to combine Flemish principles with French skill and mental agility and did a number of studies of Church men and women. But the really memorable artist of this era was Poussin, who, choosing ancient subjects, became one of the chief exponents of Classicism, which Louis XIV (who began his personal reign just four years before Poussin's death) was to admire and encourage. In the second half of the seventeenth century, the Sun King ruled supreme in art as in everything else, ably seconded by his artistic dictator Le Brun, whose influence was especially felt in the magnificent Palace of Versailles. Claude Lorrain depicted the brilliance of Mediterranean scenes; Mignard turned out

Poussin's biblical *Adoration of the Golden Calf*.
(Reproduced by courtesy of the Trustees, The National Gallery, London)

91

fashionable portraits and Van der Meulen recorded on canvas the monarch's glory and conquests. At the end of the century, artists like Largillière and Rigaud escaped a little from the influence of Le Brun and began to imitate the Naturalism of Rubens.

But this was still the age of decoration, and the *Rococo* style pervaded Watteau's delicious Regency studies of courtiers, parks, statues, fountains and clowns. Pater and Lancret copied this slightly ethereal, Colourist enre; but, about the middle of the eighteenth century François Boucher's *Boudoir* style gained supremacy, especially in court circles and with the rich burghers of Paris, while Nattier provided classical, allegorical settings for famous people and La Tour's pastel compositions represented more realistically the leaders of society. But ordinary people and things were not overlooked in the Age of the Enlightenment. Chardin shows us simple, homely folk and still-life studies of everyday objects painted with genius and, in the second half of the eighteenth century, Greuze began to set domestic scenes, often of a dramatic character and with a serious moral purpose. In a century of contrasts, moreover, it is not surprising that Fragonard chimed in with Boucher's sensual style and Chardin's homeliness while, at the end of the century, Hubert Robert painted gloomy ruins at the same time as Madame Vigée-Lebrun gave her contemporaries beautifully coloured portraits of the famous, and J. B. Regnault became so enamoured with neo-Classicism that some of his sitters look more like marble statues than men and women.

However, the best exponent of neo-Classicism was David, who lived to paint not only the French revolutionaries, but also the Emperor Napoleon. Gérard, Girodet, Ingres, Prudhon, and Gros were also very busy reflecting on canvas the glories of the Emperor and his family, whilst, of course, in an age before newsreels and television, engaged to record stirring events.

The Romantic period that followed heralded a reaction against neo-Classicism in favour of an emotional kind of Naturalism, best studied in the works of Géricault and Delacroix.

Later in the nineteenth century, a second Fontainebleau School, centred round the little village of Barbizon, was established. It is best remembered by the work of Corot, and his unmistakable skill in lighting subjects with a soft haze, and Millet, who showed us peasants at their toil. Though Millet often imparts a religious atmosphere to his studies, Courbet and Manet stressed the Naturalist trend, which continued until the time of the Impressionist painters, who made the happy discovery that, by juxtaposing dabs of light and shade they could *suggest*, rather than portray, reality. Traditional considerations like draughtsmanship and composition having

Opposite: David, Napoleon Crossing the Alps. (*The Mansell Collection*)

BONAPARTE

Manet's *Concert in the Tuileries Gardens.*

been relegated to a position of secondary importance, Impressionism represented the immediate effect made upon the artist's eye by a scene, object or person and achieved lighting effects by laying side by side contrasting touches of colour. When we think of Impressionism, we cannot ignore Monet, whose *Impression: Soleil Levant* of 1874 started the whole movement, and we must mention Boudin, Sisley, Seurat and Pissarro, as fairly orthodox exponents of the new medium.

Later when Renoir, Degas and Cézanne began to introduce their own particular ideas, the whole conception of Impressionism changed, whilst Van Gogh and Gauguin did not hesitate to introduce some *Primitivist* distortion. This last word sums up very much of the art of the twentieth century, which no longer believes in emulating photography. The neo-Impressionists, called also *Pointillists*, painted in round dots; the Wild Men (or *Fauves*), Rouault, Matisse, Derain and Dufy, rebelled in their own distinctive ways, whilst *Cubists* like Picasso and Braque worked in geo-

A Braque Cubist picture : can
you spot the mandolin ?

metrical patterns, and members of the Paris School – the Douanier Rousseau, Utrillo and Chagall – developed very distinctive styles that lead naturally to our present age of independence, rebellion, individualism and anarchy.

Looking Ahead

What will the Paris Region be like at the end of this century? 'Towards Paris 2000' was the title of an exhibition held in March 1968, revealing the planners' schemes to relieve congestion in Europe's second largest city. Paris is to expand westwards towards Normandy, which will be fed by two enormous motorways, north and south of the present city limits. The northern road will end at Le Havre and the southern arm at Caen, whilst a whole rosary of new towns will be strung out within easy access of each *autoroute*.

If you think that this is wildly futuristic and imaginative, perhaps you would care to consider a more realistic period. Remember that, since the Second World War, France has been busy peering into the future, while working out her five development plans, covering respectively the years 1947–53, 1954–57, 1958–61, 1962–65 and 1966–70. On the evidence of what has been achieved in the *past* twenty years or so, it has been possible for planners to forecast what it will be like to live in France twenty years *from now*, that is, long before the year 2000 A.D.

Planners expect the standard of living to rise more sharply than it did during the whole nineteenth century. People will spend 30 per cent more on housing and 50 per cent more on recreation, and, as a general forecast, internal consumption will increase by 300 per cent. It is hoped that scientific progress and the application of enlightened techniques to production will be able to cope with this increase. The population of France as a whole will reach sixty millions, so there will be many more mouths to feed, partly because, as the descendants of Louis Pasteur and Madame Curie conquer more and more diseases, men and women will live longer. At the same time, it is only fair to say that, with twenty million cars racing along French roads, especially at the week-ends, it is highly likely that more and more members of French families will become motoring casualties!

The family itself will change its structure; father and mother will gradually achieve equal status, and father, who traditionally rules the roost

96

in France, will, by the end of the century, be obliged to accept partnership, with all that it implies. And what of the chidren?

Education will also undergo important, if subtle, changes. Children will be taught more and more away from their home areas, often in special centres or by youth leaders. The numbers taught will undoubtedly increase in the next twenty years. In 1985, of a hundred French people aged seventeen, nearly a hundred will to go school, compared with twenty-eight in 1960 and a presumed forty-two in 1970. Again, education will be conceived on a much wider scale, embracing child, adolescent and adult alike, and using space age techniques, audio-visual methods, televison, and teaching machines. It is also envisaged that pupils will take part more in lessons by discussion and that teachers will PONTIFICATE less, and, since the upheavals of May–June 1968, it has been announced that higher education will be less 'compartmentalized'; students will be freer to pass from one 'discipline' to another at will. Moreover, even though they have unfortunately been denied the emotional and political safety-valve supplied in Britain by the university 'unions', French students may find themselves at least participating in policy decisions.

The continuing drift from the country to town will strain existing facilities, especially rail, road and air services. Luckily France has room in which to build all those extra houses, but what about thousands of new motor-cars? Will CONGESTION defeat all our plans for the future? The word 'our' is chosen with good reason. Questions of this sort, which admittedly only the future can really answer, are ours too, as indeed are most French problems.

So, at the end of this little volume, we may perhaps decide that, despite fascinating national pecularities which, heaven knows, make a trip abroad really worthwhile, we are not really very different from our nearest neighbour in Europe. The fact is, of course, that irrevocably and inevitably both nations are becoming more *European*!

Some Important Dates

B.C.

20000	Wall paintings on the caves at Lascaux
12000	The Celts, or Gauls, settled in what is now France
800	Greek invasions
600	Greeks founded Marseilles
120	Romans settled in Provence, around the Rhône
58–52	Julius Caesar conquered Gaul. From then until fifth century A.D., remained a Roman province

A.D.

350	First German invasions
496	Clovis, first king of the Franks, baptized
800	Emperor of the West, Charlemagne, baptized
987	Hugues Capet founded Capetian dynasty (Louis XVI was to be known as 'citizen Capet' after he had lost his throne in 1792)
1096–99	First Crusade
c. XI-XIIth	Great Norman and Romanesque (roman-e) edifices erected
c. XII-XIIIth	Great Gothic cathedrals built
1226–70	Saint Louis, King
1309–77	Pope in Avignon
1337–1453	One Hundred Years War
1363–1477	Dukes of Burgundy
1429	Joan of Arc relieved Orleans
1515–47	François I. Renaissance
1610–43	Louis XIII
1643–1715	Louis XIV
1661–77	Versailles redesigned
1723–74	Personal reign of Louis XV
1789	Great Revolution breaks out
1793	Louis XVI guillotined
1799	Bonaparte comes to power
1804–15	Bonaparte becomes Emperor Napoleon
1815	Battle of Waterloo
1852–70	Napoleon III (nephew of Napoleon) emperor

1870	Third Republic
1914–18	First World War
1939–45	Second World War
June 1940	De Gaulle makes his appeal from London
June 6 1944	Allies disembark in Normandy
1958	Beginning of the Fifth Republic

Glossary

ACCREDIT	To send out, with authority
AESTHETIC	Artistic
AMALGAMATION	The joining together or merging of things or people
APÉRITIF	A French word for an appetizer, usually made of alcohol
AUTOCRACY	Repressive, or absolute, government
AUTOMATION	Industrial processes implying the minimum reliance upon workers
COIFFE	A French female regional head-dress of lace
CONGEST	To cause partial blockage or obstruction by an unusual flow
CONTROVERSIAL	Leading to argument
FRANCOPHILE	Lover of things French
GARGANTUAN	Enormous. Gargantua was a giant in the work of Rabelais
GASTRONOME	Good judge in cookery
GENDARME	French provincial, national policeman, living in barracks and under a kind of military discipline – not to be confused with the *agent*, or town policeman
GUILLOTINE	Beheading machine, reputed to be humane compared with the axe!
HEXAGON	A six-sided geometrical figure
HIERARCHY	An organization in grades
HOLOGRAPH	Individual manuscript
HYDROELECTRIC	Developing electricity by water power
INSOLVENCY	Inability to pay one's debts
INTREPID	Rash, daring

LAMINATED	Beaten or rolled into thin plates or layers
LIGATURE	Bind or tie
MAQUIS	An irregular armed force in woods and thickets
PEDANTIC	One who overrates book-learning
PHENOMENAL	Colossal, exceptional
PONTIFICATE	To speak from on high
PROPHETIC	Foretelling the future
RATIFY	Confirm
REGIME	System of government
RENAISSANCE	Revival of arts and letters under the influence of Ancient Greece and Rome. It took place in France in the late fifteenth and early sixteenth centuries
RURAL	Pertaining to the countryside
SEPTUAGENARIAN	Aged between seventy and eighty
STERILIZE	Render free from harmful bacteria or germs
TESTAMENT	Document conveying a person's last wishes
UNIVERSAL SUFFRAGE	Every citizen over a certain age having the right to vote in elections
VERTIGINOUS	Enough to make one dizzy
VOCIFERATE	To shout out